1500 Years of Christian I

Nicholas Roscarrock's Hymn
to His Patroness Saint Endelienta

Sweet Saint Endelienta, virgin pure,
Daughter of Prince and Saint, yea, Sister dear
of many Saints which stoutly did endure
Conflicts in world with sinners living here:
Vouchsafe, Sweet Saint, my Patroness to be,
To pray for him who humbly prays to thee.

To thee, who being born of royal blood,
Having the world as 'twere at thy own will,
Left all to follow God, true Sovereign Good,
who only was thy soul to fill,
Daunting the world, the flesh, the fiend and sin,
for life well led, an endless life to win.

For which a Saint thou worthily art crowned
In heaven above with everlasting bliss,
and here on earth below likewise renowned
where to thy name a Church erected is,
even there where thy life did lead and leave,
and where I, wretch, true life did first receive.

For in that Church a Christian I became
and of Christ's Church a Member first to be,
And also was Confirmed in the same.
For which I thank my God, and pray to thee
this work to further in thy Church begun
With prayers that I my race may rightly run:

To imitate in part thy virtues rare —
Thy faith, hope, charity, thy humble mind,
Thy chasteness, meekness, and thy diet spare,
And that which in this world is hard to find:
the love which thou to enemy didst show,
reviving him who sought thy overthrow.

Unto the Three and One praise show for this;
And all thy fellow saints with me request
that I may shun to sin and do amiss,
bewail sins past, and follow God's behest:
Grant me this grace, good God, whose might is most,
Thrice blessed Father, Son and Holy Ghost.

Rest on the Flight into Egypt. Harold Harvey, following time-honoured custom, places a contemporary Our Lady and Saint Joseph with the Child Jesus in the local setting of West Penwith moorland.

THE SAINTS OF CORNWALL

1500 Years of
Christian Landscape

Catherine Rachel John

TABB HOUSE
Padstow

Published 2001
Tabb House, 7 Church Street, Padstow,
Cornwall, PL28 8BG

First edition published 1981 by Lodenek Press
and reprinted 1986 by Dyllansow Truran

Hardback ISBN 1 873951 27 2
Paperback   1 873951 39 6

British Library Cataloguing-in-Publication Data:
a catalogue record of this title is available from
the British Library.

CONTENTS

Page

AUTHOR'S ACKNOWLEDGEMENTS

If I were to mention everyone who has in one way or another contributed to this book, it would be necessary to detail half a life-time's history. I must refer the reader to the many allusions and references, from blessed Nicholas Roscarrock at the beginning to the beautiful end-piece, and assure the living and the physically dead that I am properly grateful.

Listing names is not always practicable, and I should like to mention collectively the rectors of Breton parishes and the clergy of Catholic and Church of England parishes in Cornwall who have been so patient with queries and the invasion of their churches for the purpose of taking photographs. Similarly, my thanks to various Methodist ministers, as also to lay folk of a variety of Christian confessions, for on the spot aid and advice.

Donald Rawe gave me the opportunity to write this book. Graham Sandercock was an ever patient teacher of Cornish; transport to places which I could not otherwise reach has also been provided, and help with details of research, typing and proof-reading especially by Jean Moore. So it goes on, 'line upon line, here a little, there a little'; which must not lead me to overlook my final acknowledgement: to the land and people of Kernow.

Picture Credits

I am grateful for the provision of photographs to the following: Ron Chapman, H. J. Ingrey, the monks of Fort Augustus Abbey, Derek Holmes, Stanley George, Frank Parkinson, Hamish Johnson-Stewart, David Cook, and the late Ray Bishop, and to John Webb for the Chi/Rho and Celtic cross designs, and Cornish-Latin lettering.

LIST OF ILLUSTRATIONS

PART I

The Historical Setting

Hymn to Saint Petroc

Saintly Confessor of the faith of Jesus,
He whom in Cornwall venerate the faithful,
Spurning earth's pleasures, bound himself to follow
Holy Religion.

Godly and prudent was our holy Petroc,
Peaceful and learned. To his faithful preaching
Constantine harkened: even beasts drew near him
Slocked by his kindness.

Sowing the Gospel where the sea and river
Mingle their waters, long he dwelt among us,
Passing to Bodmin, there to God his Maker
Rendered his being.

Now dwelleth Petroc with the Saints in glory,
But, ever mindful of the seed he planted,
Though parted from us, poureth supplications,
Pleading for Cornwall.

Wherefore in chorus thankfully to Godward
Raise we our voices, loud in jubilation;
Praise be to Father, Son, and Holy Spirit,
Now and for ever.

Athelstan Riley

THE HISTORICAL SETTING

THE CORNISH CHURCHTOWN

A large number of places in Cornwall are named after saints, the saints to whom the churches, forming the centre of the community, are dedicated. The uninstructed visitor from England or across the seas, who expects simply the farthest west of the English counties, meets, as soon as he has crossed the River Tamar, not only St John or even St Germans but St Mellion or St Erney. He may stay in St Austell or, more probably, St Ives. If he is interested in more aspects of his host country than sand, sea and, with luck, sun, he may wonder what is the significance of Lanhydrock other than being a well-kept National Trust property, or notice not only Perranporth but Perranzabuloe.

Of course it is not only a question of the names of village or township. Tintagel was, or perhaps was not, King Arthur's Castle. But, having clambered up the steps – so like the ascent of Purgatory in Dante's *Divine Comedy* – to the magnificent headland, what is this prize which is offered to us as well as castle and sea-scape – the Celtic monastery? When I was young I used to sit on Mousehole rocks with my Mother, who was younger in heart than I, and watch the white gulls settle on St Clement's Island in the evening. The saint is hanging out his washing, we would remark, and what a lot of handkerchiefs he uses! But who was Saint Clement, of the island from which Mousehole was anciently named: Porth Enys (Island Harbour, Island Cove)?

What of the two Looes, with Saint Mary and Saint Nicholas, hardly Celtic saints; or, to move to later times, King Charles the Martyr at Falmouth parish church, John Wesley commemorated in a sculpture over the doorway of Altarnun's first Methodist church, Saint Cuthbert Mayne celebrated in pilgrimage at Launceston? These are questions that may be asked by Cornish people as well as others, who have been ill-equipped by what passes for the teaching of the history of our communities, in school and out of it.

THE PATTERN OF THIS BOOK

PART I of the book deals with the fundamental setting and historical outline, mainly of the early centuries from the fifth AD, though it also comments on the Middle Ages and on later times. This will include some consideration of what is meant by the term 'saint', and various related points, and of customs particularly relevant to Cornwall.

1

1. Remains of the Celtic monastery, near the castle on Tintagel 'island'.

Part II deals in alphabetical order with what are usually termed the Cornish Saints, though, as will be seen, few of them were actually Cornish by birth: the term Celtic is useful here.

Part III introduces, also in alphabetical order, various saints to whom churches and chapels were dedicated mainly during mediaeval times.

Part IV presents a review of changes and developments since the mid-sixteenth century.

The aim overall is to give the reader a living understanding of the Christian landscape of Cornwall, as he walks in it after more than fifteen hundred years of history.

Such sections cannot of course be regarded as hard and fast divisions; sometimes it is a moot point as to where an entry should go, or it is not clear for simple historical reasons. An outstanding example can be found under the name of Dominick in Part III: this is not one Dominick but two, and the history of the dedications runs right through from early Celtic times to our own century. The course to follow, then, is to try another section if the sought-after name is not found in one, with the guidance of the introductory notes to Parts II and III.

The Isles of Scilly are not part of Cornwall, but their history is linked to it and they cannot be wholly omitted from a book of this sort. A Scillonian sketch map with notes is to be found on pp. 135-137.

The Title has been expressed precisely as the 'Saints of Cornwall' rather than the 'Cornish Saints' for two reasons, both of which emerge from what has been said above. Most of those saints whom the Cornish rightly feel as especially of their land and people were not in fact born in Cornwall, although they usually lived in the country, either temporarily or permanently. Moreover, there is no reason to deprive Cornish life of those citizens of the City of God who have come to be venerated during the many centuries after the Celtic Christian foundation period.

CELTIC CORNWALL

Roman Britain

It is hard to grasp historical perspectives imaginatively. At about the time of the birth of Christ, the Roman Empire, with already some four hundred years of Republic behind it, was to last in western Europe a further four hundred years (and in the East of course a great deal longer). This is about the same length of time as that from the reign of Queen Elizabeth I to Queen Elizabeth II. Yet the latter period seems far longer to us, not so much because there is more known about it as because we are taught – adults and children alike – so much more about it.

In particular, for our theme, it is not commonly understood how widely Christianity had spread, and how deeply rooted and highly organized it was by the time the Emperor Constantine the Great, realizing its value and importance, gave it full recognized status in the Empire in AD 313. There were still to follow about a hundred years of coherent Roman life; and so it was that the Christian Church and communities were prepared not simply to sit out the chaos that eventually came, but to carry on civilized life where it had not been wholly overwhelmed, to rebuild, and sometimes to create quite new communities.

There is no general shortage of information about this period, but unfortunately not much is known of British Christianity. There is a tradition that Pope St Eleutherius sent the first missionaries to Britain, at the request of a local chieftain, at the end of the second century. Rather less than a hundred years later, probably in the persecutions which followed Diocletian's attempts to tighten up discipline in the Empire, Britain had her early martyrs. The names of three have come down to us: Julius and Aaron who were put to death at Caerleon (modern south-east Wales) and the more famous Alban. He was a pagan who gave shelter to a Christian priest, was converted by him, and gladly allowed himself to be arrested and executed in his stead. Alban's tomb was preserved at what was then the Roman Verulamium – and in due time his shrine gave rise to the city of St Albans – a remarkable survival from early British or Celtic life – through pagan Saxon invasion and settlement, into the flowering of English Christianity.

With the new freedom of the Church in the early fourth century came the meetings or councils of bishops and others concerned with the teachings and organization of a body which now stretched from Persia to Spain, from North

Africa to Britain. Names of British bishops are found among those who attended the Council of Arles in southern Gaul (Provence) in 314, at Sardica (Sofia in modern Bulgaria) in about 343, and at Rimini (Italy) in 359. How much appreciated were not only the Roman roads but all the amenities of the *Pax Romana*!

Archaeological discoveries show us some signs of Christianity, such as the little church at Silchester (north Hampshire) and the mosaic floor in the villa at Hinton St Mary, Dorset, with its picture of Christ in the centre. On this, too, we see the Chi/Rho cross, or sacred monogram, found also at the villa at Chedworth (Gloucestershire) and sometimes marked on such domestic articles as dishes and spoons. (See p. 138.)

Transition

The Roman Empire did not disintegrate overnight. In any case we are here concerned with the Empire in the West. Perhaps we too often forget that a form of the Christian Eastern Empire continued until its capital, Constantinople, was captured by the Turks in 1453. (Visitors to Landulph church by the Tamar, north of Saltash, can see a brass marking the burial-place of Theodore Paleologus, a descendant of the brother of the last emperor, Constantine XI.)

Nor was the Empire forgotten in the West. Charlemagne's attempt from AD 800 to revive a Christian Roman Empire – more truly a great confederation of states - was to play a major role in European history right up to the final destruction of the Austro-Hungarian Empire in the First World War, and has influenced the thinking that has gone into the formation of the European Union and the Council of Europe.

What is called the fall of the Roman Empire was a process so varied and so chaotic that it cannot be described in brief. It is to be remembered, for instance, that the 'barbarian' invaders were not all savage pagans intent only on destruction and spoils. Some of those taking an especial interest in Italy had already been in contact with Roman civilization and were Christians, even if of a heretical body, with leaders genuinely concerned to maintain the stability of Rome.

The picture, however, for the British Isles and neighbouring Gaul is rather simpler. Here we find not a relatively cohesive development of one form of community structure into another, but the break that is made by the invasion of peoples who totally overwhelmed earlier, civilized ways of life. In the face of this, it was the Celtic peoples who maintained and developed direct traditions from the already partially Christian past.

The settlement of Angles, Saxons and Jutes in what became Angle-land, England, was not a speedy or unopposed affair. Basically, it covered the fifth and the sixth centuries. This was the time of the original 'King' Arthur. He has become far and away the most famous of the leaders who inherited the age-old civilization of Rome and Greece, with the inspiration of the Christian world view, but who had to struggle against the tribes of Germanic-speaking peoples, after the hard-pressed Roman authorities said, in 410, that Britain must fend for herself in military matters.

It is impossible to determine precisely how much of what was British remained where the early English settled. It is inconceivable that all Britons of the east and south either fled west and north or were massacred. The invaders had no means of understanding the civilization they met; the stately buildings of the Roman cities and towns fell into decay and most of them gradually disappeared. But the barbarians used those towns for centres of their own, and thus we still have York and London, Chester and Chichester and Exeter, and many others. Some kind of give and take, too, is implied in the Celtic words which found their way into the early English language, notably those to do with the land which the tribes were now inhabiting: rivers named Avon, for example, from the Celtic word (modern Welsh *afon*, modern Cornish *avon*) meaning simply 'river'.

It is, however, certain that many of the original inhabitants did flee to join their fellows living in the north-west and in what we now call Wales, Somerset, Devon and Cornwall. Considerable numbers from the south-west crossed the sea to settle in that part of Gaul called by the Romans Armorica, but which from this time took on the name of the land they had come from, and so became little Britain or Brittany. Others went to northern Spain. This movement is usually ascribed to the pressure of the Saxon invasions, and if we think of that pressure as being – in the far south-west – psychological rather than physical, then it surely played its part. But it seems that fear of another kind of enemy was also impelling people to flee – a form of bubonic plague was ravaging western Britain and Ireland at this time.

Only very gradually were the various parts of the Celtic world cut off from each other, shrinking into isolated sections. Sea routes between them were main links, not barriers. As for the land, it was perfectly common to go from Cornwall to Wales, for instance, via north Devon and Somerset, crossing the River Severn in what we now call Gloucestershire. Similarly it was possible to go from Wales north into that Celtic area of which we have still a reminder in the name of Cumberland – recognized by the early English as the land of those people who called themselves, as the Welsh still do today, Cymru. There were of course a number of distinct kingdoms – including in the south-west peninsula, that of Dumnonia, which lasted, in ever diminishing size, into the early tenth century.

Cardinal Figures

In this period, as so often happens, there were certain pivotal figures on whom turned development from past into present and present into future. They might be called, in imitation of the 'hinge', or cardinal, virtues and certain central offices in the organization of the Catholic Church, cardinal figures. For Western Europe as a whole Saint Benedict with his twin sister Saint Scholastica and Saint Severinus (better known as Boethius) should be mentioned. The following notes on those of especial interest in our areas here may serve as pivots on which to turn an understanding of the period.

Saint Martin of Tours. The fourth century builder of active, self-reliant Christian life, spreading an influence far beyond Roman Gaul. He did a great deal to prepare Christian communities for the struggles, endeavours and creative work to come. (See his entry in Part III.)

Saint Germanus of Auxerre was born in the later fourth century and died in 448; a champion of the integrity of Christian life and faith. Of particular interest for us because he taught Saint Patrick and later consecrated him bishop, possibly taught and ordained Saint Illtud, visited Britain twice, and was concerned for the well-being of Armorica – early Brittany. (See his entry in Part II.)

Clovis, King of the Franks and Queen Clotilde. Franks – Germanic peoples reckoned to be even more savage than the Huns – flooded into Roman Gaul. The great Frankish King, Clovis, married a Christian wife – Saint Clotilde, and his acceptance of Christianity in 496 began the transformation of the lands across the Channel from Britain. (Brittany also played its part; see Mullion in Part II.)

Saint Ninian. The son of a British chieftain, he went to Rome where he received the light of Christian-Classical culture, and brought it back to his Candida Casa, the Fair White House, at what is now Whithorn in South Galloway. This became a centre of life and inspiration for what we call southern Scotland, northern Ireland, the Isle of Man, the Lake District. He died in about 432.

Saint Patrick. A near contemporary of Ninian, he lived from about 385 to 461. A Christian from the west coast of Britain, he was carried to Ireland (never under Roman rule) by pirates. After his escape and ordination to the priesthood he returned as a missionary – one of the wisest and noblest in the history of the Church, and the virtual founder of the Classical-Christian-Celtic civilization which was Ireland's glory.

Saint Bridgid lived from about 450 to 523, Saint Patrick's successor, a great abbess and founder of nunneries, and a great personality. She has been revered not only in Ireland but also the Isle of Man, in Scotland, Wales, England; in later times her veneration has gone right round the world, reaching Australia and New Zealand.

Saint Illtud. Also of a new generation; he lived in the fifth to early sixth century. His monastery at Llanilltud Fawr – Llantwit Major in south Wales –

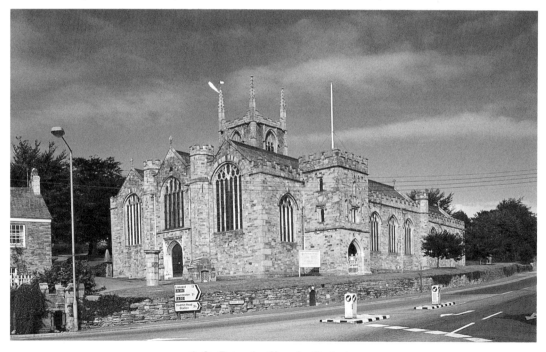

2. St Petroc's Church, Bodmin

flourished under the inspiration of its abbot, who was described as 'the most learned in the Scriptures, in philosophy, and in all the subjects of a liberal education'. It was one of the chief centres of education, religious training and missionary activity.

Saint David. The most famous of the Welsh saints, and a great founder of monasteries in the generation that followed Illtud; the dates are uncertain. Best known of course is what came to be called Saint David's in far west Wales, where Irish saints, among many people, came for religious education. (See Part II.)

Saint Samson. From a child, a pupil of Saint Illtud's monastic school, and one of Illtud's greatest disciples. He is remembered in Wales and Cornwall, but above all he is one of the foundation saints of Christian Brittany. He lived from about 490 to 565. (See his entry in Part II.)

Saint Petroc. The most distinguished gift from sixth century Wales to south-west Britain. His fame and influence spread widely, and did not wane in mediaeval times. He is the greatest foundation saint of Cornwall. (See his entry in Part II.)

Saint Columba. The Irish saint who took up the work in Scotland; born about 521, he died in 597, the year when Saint Augustine and his missionary monks from Rome landed in Kent. From Columba's centre on Iona, Christian life spread to Lindisfarne and to the pagan Angles settled in northern England. Not to be confused with Saint Columban, the foremost of those Irish missionaries of about the same period who created centres of Christian civilization on the European continent.

CELTIC SAINTS

The work of such outstanding people partly explains the flourishing of Christian activity from the fifth century, all through the sixth and on into the seventh century, though in the nature of things this Age of the Saints needs to be seen in the light of the Spirit who 'breathes where He will . . .'

Religion is of necessity a political and social concern. People live in organized communities, and public leadership on fundamental matters of belief and behaviour is as important in these as in other matters of community life. At the same time the profoundly personal, as well as general and universal, implications of Christianity mean that it is vital for formation in religious life to work upwards through the community as well as downwards.

This is what marks out the labours and journeyings of the Celtic saints for especial honour. The familiar missionary pattern occurs of course: the conversion of local rulers, through whom their subjects are led into the Christian fold. But it is not so marked in the Celtic world. Rather, we witness many individuals, especially from Ireland and Wales, making their journeys from their original homes to settle in new places. Here they create centres of Christian life among the people. When the work is established, sometimes they move on, sometimes it is to be presumed they remain for life.

They would be working on the whole among people with some inheritance of Classical civilization and a certain acquaintance with Christianity, but in great danger of losing touch with both. The impact of this great array of men and women can be seen in the places named after them in all the Celtic countries of northern Europe, not least in Cornwall and Brittany.

Style of Life, Work and Worship

To speak of the work of individuals is not to give an impression of isolation, far from it. We have records not only of close friendships but of families engaged in the work of building Christian communities. The Celtic Saints provide a most illuminating illustration of the full vocation of the Christian, in contradiction of assumptions on the lay side that 'apostolic' endeavours can comfortably be left to priests, monks and nuns, and, on the clerical, that lay people are not to be trusted with them.

Priests, Monks and Nuns. That a number of the men were ordained priests is obvious enough. But shared activities are apparent, as we see for instance in the life of Saint Samson where, before leaving Wales for Cornwall, he 'goes to see his mother and his aunt, and he consecrates the churches which they have already built'.

Monks were not usually priests. The custom of ordaining 'choir monks' grew up later in the Western Church; Saint Benedict himself, the greatest monastic founder and one of the greatest influences in all European civilization, was probably never ordained to the priesthood. The Celtic style of monastic life was very different from the ordered Benedictine, even allowing for the fact that with time complexities came which were not envisaged by Benedict and his sister Scholastica. In the Celtic church groups of men and women, friends or relations, would come together, each individual living in his own little cell or cottage, but meeting for the necessary small-scale husbandry, for some meals, and for communal prayer in the chapel. The pattern is evident in the remains of such community buildings now so well preserved on Tintagel headland.

This is similar in type to early monastic life in the eastern Mediterranean countries and Christian north Africa, and to that which was popular in and around Rome from the fourth century. There would be links between such areas through 'schools' of monastic life, such as that of Saint Martin at Tours, but there was not an over-all system, because the little monasteries grew out of local conditions. As is to be expected, this gave rise to considerable variety even in the Celtic monasteries alone, not only in size and organization but strictness of life. Perhaps too much has been made of the Celtic devout man standing up to his neck in a stream while he sings the seven Penitential Psalms:

> If Thou, O Lord, shall observe iniquities,
> Lord, who shall endure it?
> With Thee there is merciful forgiveness,
> And by reason of Thy law I have waited for Thee,
>   O Lord . . .

We may also remember that when Saint Samson first came to Cornwall and approached the monastery of Docco, now St Kew, he was asked by the wisest of the brothers and their spokesman not to stay with them. They were anxious lest his presence disturb, rather than constructively help, a community which admitted that 'we come short of our former practice'. The Saint was not shocked; he was impressed by their honesty.

Abbot-Bishops. It is hard to imagine an organized life which is different from that in which we have grown up. Neither priest nor bishop is made by his presiding over a parish or diocese with distinct boundaries: the function of each is sacramental, a particular and fundamental (but not exclusive) bearer of divine grace and authority for the people. Thus in the Celtic life of that time there were multifold small religious centres, served by priests who were members of the small local monastery, ordained for that purpose. The higher authority would lie in the abbot of a larger monastery, or one central to the neighbourhood, who would most likely be consecrated bishop. The great majority of these naturally remained in one place; but there were those who were called to follow the travels of Celtic missionaries. Samson, for example, was deacon, priest, and abbot in south Wales; but once consecrated bishop he left for Cornwall, and went on to his great work in Brittany. The bishop is vital for the foundation and general growth of the Christian community because of his special sacramental powers and teaching authority. This seems almost unaccountably to have been neglected in much later missionary activity, which too often depended on a constant supply of priests and nuns from elsewhere, artificially supporting communities which should have been building themselves around a local bishop.

3. Abbot-Bishop's mitre of Celtic design made in recent times and in the position of Fort Augustus Abbey, Scotland.

'They reared their lodges in the wilderness . . .' The hunger of the Celtic people for that communion with God experienced in solitude among the glories of nature, is vividly expressed in the life of Saint Petroc. A monastic founder, he was also strongly impelled to lead the life of a hermit in remote areas when he was able to withdraw from commitments to his communities. As with other saints, such commitments could develop in his very solitude. The foundation of Bodmin came about when brethren were attracted to share the holy life of Petroc in his cell on the edge of the lonely moor. But at any peaceful spot, let alone an island, there might be found a man or woman living temporarily or permanently.

Again we have to try to forget our assumptions, this time about a simple division between lay and clerical that is of fairly recent date, and is at present being re-examined. Clear and definite enough are the characteristics of the ordained priest, of men and women living under formal vows in the 'families' of monks and nuns, of married people with their form of vow and family. It is not so easy to attach a label, for example, to the man or woman who lives alone, pursuing a life of prayer and study which leads out into apostolic work, with or without a vow of dedicated virginity. Yet it was men and women such as these who created numerous Christian communities in Cornwall. This becomes more credible when we recall that the sacramental power of carrying on the Christian community resides in human beings as such. Baptism not simply may, but must, be conferred by a lay person if a priest or deacon is not available, while to a marriage, in any case, he gives only the Church's witness and blessing – the union conferred upon each other by bride and groom is not invalidated if for a genuine reason it cannot take place before an ordained minister.

Signs of the Celtic Saints

I and my white Pangur
has each his special art;
his mind is set on catching mice,
mine is on my own craft . . .

*The opening of a poem in the
MS of an early Irish monk*

What, however, probably happened is that when Pangur appeared with a mouse in his teeth, his master removed it, with courteous apology to the cat, and saw it safely off home. The exquisite respect (extending in traditional tales even to dragons) for all the things and creatures of God's creation, is a mark, not unique, but very notable, of the Celtic saints.

Signs and Wonders. God's creatures responded to the Celtic saints as they do to those who respect, because they love, them. All this is sometimes illustrated in symbolic stories, such as that depicted in the mediaeval glass in St Neot church where, the saint's oxen having been stolen, stags come to offer their services at the plow.

It is necessary to distinguish between 'legends' of the saints in the exact meaning of written accounts, intended to be factual records, and the mass of legends in the common sense of the term: stories, oral and written down, accumulated over the centuries - like the difference between historical accounts of Mary Queen of

Scots, and the numberless stories and poems which have been composed about her, in their own way bearing witness to her existence though ranging from largely fact to mainly fictional romance.

But it is in the seminal tradition of the signs and wonders of the Bible in both Old and New Testaments, that saints live. Because a thing is a 'miracle', it does not mean that it did not happen (which has been demonstrated as far as physical science can ever go in such matters at Lourdes in modern times). Everywhere the saints see the workings of God, though some events may seem more startling to lookers-on than others: 'When Samson prayed for the third night, at nearly midnight he saw a light from Heaven appear before him, and he heard a longed-for voice, out of the light, saying sweetly to him: "Distress yourself no further, chosen servant of God, for behold, you will solve this question at which you are labouring". . .'

Holy Wells. While very few remains of church buildings survive in Cornwall from those times, mainly because newer and larger churches were erected on the same spot, everywhere are to be found the wells, most commonly named after the local saint. In later times they tended to decline into the innocent enough wishing wells (white magic, not black) and sometimes to be neglected altogether. But in the network of scattered Christian communities the well is simply the basic source of life. Water is necessary for physical survival, let alone cleanliness, health and comfort; and it is necessary for baptism.

4. Modern protection for Saint Constantine's well on Trevose golf course.

5. Going down into the waters of baptism, as shown in Saint Keyne's holy well (restored).

No doubt in many places a well already existed, perhaps associated with some pagan spirit; in others, one was constructed to channel a spring. Nor need we discount the essential truth of stories in which saints are divinely led to the discovery of such sources of water.

What is fully in the Celtic Christian tradition, a combination of the classic Christianity of the Continent and what might be called the Celtic style, is this very marked sacramental intermingling of the natural and the supernatural. Water is not brought from somewhere and put into a font; it is living water, like that of the River Jordan. Moreover, the well may be so constructed that the people go down steps into it – for, as witnessed in many ancient baptisteries, baptism is both a cleansing and going down into the death of Christ and rising with him in the new life. At the same time, the villagers come to the well to fill their cloam jugs, while the children dip their hands to gather drops of water for their play.

Bells. We are accustomed to the idea of church bells, calling people to service and, in the older traditions, marking the daily hours of prayer and therefore the times of day for those round about. Celtic saints, travelling through the countryside and gathering listeners for their preaching, carried and rang hand bells. These again were much more than plain articles of convenience. There is, in any case, something mysteriously impressive about bells (as is depicted so vividly in Dorothy L. Sayers' *The Nine Tailors*), and the bell of a saint was treasured after his death and might be used in community rituals. Saint Petroc's Bell was kept at Bodmin, for instance, and legal agreements were ratified with a

6. The bell of Paul Aurelian, enshrined in his cathedral of St Pol de Léon in Brittany.

hand on the bell, in the same manner as touching the Gospels or a crucifix.

Such small objects were usually lost or destroyed, with time and change. But at least two are preserved in Brittany. (See Meryadoc and Paul Aurelian, Part II.)

CELTS AND THE EARLY ENGLISH

'Celt' is a convenient term for the main body of non-Anglo-Saxon inhabitants of the British Isles, although of course it is an over-simplification. Contrary to popular assumption, the small dark people to be met with in Cornwall and elsewhere are survivors of an earlier Bronze Age people, often called Iberians; Celts tend to be taller, and more fair.

The regularization of relations between the Celtic people in the British Isles and the newer Germanic settlers gradually came about with the conversion of these early English to Christianity, giving a cohesion of world outlook and a greater communion of cultural interest. This of course was not solely the work of Saint Augustine and his fellow Benedictines who came to what is now Kent in 597. (He found a little church already there; see Martin in Part III.) Very important was the Irish Saint Columba's monastic foundation on the Island of Iona in the north-west, and the foundation on Lindisfarne in the north-east by Saint Aidan, a monk of Iona.

It is well known that Augustine, who showed less than Roman courtesy, clashed with leaders of the Celtic Christians over questions of discipline. Of varying importance for the good order of the Church, there were matters which on the one hand we might think best left to local usage, such as the form of tonsure to be applied to the head of a monk; and on the other, the need for general agreement in the universal Church for the date of the Easter celebration. We have indications of Celtic saints and others going to Rome when they could, but, especially because of the chaos in France, the British Celts had become rather out of touch with their fellow Christians. We have here the beginning of a process of gradual sorting out, as Christian English influence grew stronger politically, and contacts with the Continent stabilized and grew more open.

South-west Britain

Here, a fairly clear pattern can be discerned. In the year 704, for instance, some hundred and fifty years after Columba landed in Iona, a hundred odd years after the coming of the Benedictine monks from Rome, and some sixty years after the founding of the monastery on Lindisfarne, the Abbot of Malmesbury in Dorset writes a letter to Gerent, King of Dumnonia. This sets out the date at which Easter should be celebrated. A year later, Ine, King of the West Saxons, appoints this same Aldhelm, saint, scholar and poet, to be the first Bishop of Sherborne. At the same time, the capable Ine, esteemed for his Code of Law, is pushing westwards. Gerent was ruling in an already shrunken Dumnonia, and by the time of Ine's death, Devon, as it came to be called, was being firmly anglicized.

Somerset had already been largely occupied. One of the most striking examples of the difference in relations, even after battle and conquest, is found in the treatment of the Abbey of Glastonbury, already a distinguished Celtic foundation. First, we see here King Ine's work again, in re-forming it, as is to be expected, along the lines of Saxon monastic life. In due course, the great Saint Dunstan gave it the full Benedictine Rule or order of life, and so it continued until 1539 and the execution of its last abbot on Glastonbury Tor. It was perhaps the greatest religious and educational centre in England, and one always conscious of its inheritance of the ancient history of Britain. (See also Kea in Part II, and Dunstan in Part III.)

Cornwall

We can trace the gradual assumption of control by the West Saxons, partly by forcible, partly by peaceful, means. A definite date is 838, when King Egbert of Wessex won a decisive victory over Cornish forces, who had made the classic mistake of allying themselves with one enemy (pagan Danish marauders) in defence against another.

From this time, Cornwall seems to have been effectively under West Saxon rule, as we see from the will of King Alfred, 899, which refers to lands in Cornwall. These were not the only sort of contacts, as we see again with the great King Alfred, who collected Christian scholars from the European continent and whose close friend and biographer was Asser, a Welsh monk from the flourishing religious centre of St David's. A bishop at both Sherborne and Exeter, it is Asser who tells of Alfred's visit to the shrine of Saint Gueryr while on a hunting holiday in Cornwall; how he prayed there, and was healed of a sickness. (See under Neot in Part II.)

The Settlement by King Athelstan. Far more than simply a King of Wessex, in 925 not only was Athelstan crowned King of the middle English Mercia, which extended his authority to some degree over the Welsh, the north Britons and the people now calling themselves Scots, but he also took a considerable role in Continental affairs. (He was godfather to Alan of Brittany, and helped him to recover his lands after he had been forced to flee to Athelstan's court.)

Athelstan was also a helper of the poor, the enslaved and the young, and a patron of piety and learning. It is not surprising, then, that he was largely responsible for a reorganization of church life in Cornwall. Following the pattern learned by the early English from developments on the Continent, the ordering of parish and diocese into definite geographical areas was encouraged. Monastic houses were treated as quite distinct bodies, though it was common enough for one to be closely associated with a cathedral. The King was concerned about continuity. He founded his Cornish bishopric at the ancient settlement of St Germans (see also Germanus in Part II), and chose a Cornishman, Conan, to be the first of its new bishops; perhaps he was already abbot-bishop of the Celtic monastery there, the existence of which Athelstan respected. At St Buryan, in West Penwith, he was responsible for changing the Celtic-style monastery into a college or community of priests, or canons, a very ancient form of religious life which has always maintained its popularity. This he substantially endowed, and it continued to flourish throughout the succeeding centuries. Similarly, he left his mark by reorganizations at Probus and Padstow.

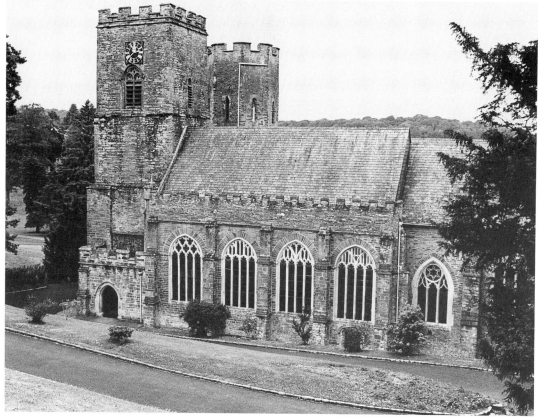

7. St Germans, one of the historic centres of Cornish Christianity.

In the time of Athelstan there were still numbers of the old British inhabitants active in eastern Dumnonia, notably in the Exeter area. It was this King who compelled the West Britons to accept the River Tamar as their boundary. It may have looked like oppression then, but the Cornish of today might be glad of an Athelstan to uphold this boundary.

Further Developments. Athelstan's work was not a single sweep of change. For a while there still seem to have been other bishops in Cornwall, notably at Bodmin monastery. However, a further step was taken by the English king, Saint Edward the Confessor, when he authorized the centralization of the bishopric for the western lands at Exeter. The Normans continued the practice of making very large episcopal sees – for no good reason that can be seen: many ancient dioceses were and are quite small, and more convenient. In Cornwall there was continued growth of collegiate churches, with the parish and other churches maintained by priests living in community.

Loss and Gain – and Growth. It is impossible not to regret the passing of ways of life and worship that sprang from the heart of a people. But, at the same time, it would be quite unfair to put it down simply to a tyrannous political and social process on the part of the English. There are rhythms of times and seasons in human life, as in that of nature, and the greatness of the whole Celtic Christian world could not have been maintained indefinitely. Wales and Ireland and

Scotland, the Isle of Man and Brittany were adopting and adapting all kinds of things from the burgeoning civilization of Christian Europe, in which church organization played its part as an essential structure.

This does not, however, mean that the past is a dead thing, at best a topic for pious historical analysis: quite the reverse. The seasons come round again. If there is one period with which the twentieth century can be compared rationally, it is that of the fifth century; the emergence from an old civilization into a probably long period of spiritual, social and political incoherence, with the Christian Church holding and building the bridges. What may be called Celtic-style Christianity has much to offer our times.

THE MIDDLE AGES

Like the 'Renaissance', the term 'Middle Ages' is one which it is hard to do without. But both are so misused that it would be a happy thing to banish them, with 'feudal', from speech and writing for a generation, thus giving people a chance to think freshly.

This book is not primarily concerned with mediaeval times in Cornwall. However, Part III deals with mainly mediaeval church dedications; Cornwall cannot be deprived of those saints who are not Celtic. The observations which follow are intended as brief aids to an understanding of the period. It is to be assumed that readers of a book of this kind are not concerned with 'mediaeval' as an indiscriminate term of abuse for things disliked or little comprehended.

Scale and Diversity

As with ancient Rome, as with early England, we have to envisage a long period. In the British Isles we can conveniently start with 1066 and the Norman Conquest; we could end possibly with the coming of the Tudors in 1485, though more significant dates might be suggested such as 1538 in Cornwall, when work on the rebuilding and adornment of Saint Mary Magdalene's Church at Launceston stopped dead.

During the Middle Ages Christendom embraced all Europe; Asia Minor as part of the eastern Christian Roman Empire until it went down before the Muslim invasions; the Holy Land in principle, and in practice during the successful period of the Crusades; also those great areas of Catholic Christianity, Ukraine and Lithuania, which later became absorbed into a more or less totalitarian Russia. Christian North Africa had already been lost.

Unity in Diversity. The cleavage between the Christianity of the west and of the east, with its roots in cultural and political history, had become increasingly apparent. The attempt to heal it in the fifteenth century met with little success, but there are some bodies of the Christian eastern traditions which maintain their allegiance to Rome. Moreover, whatever the sometimes subtle matters of doctrine and discipline in contention between East and West, there was (and is) not only a shared inheritance of beliefs from classic Christian times, taught with authority and definition, but a mutual recognition of the Sacraments.

In western Christendom itself the diversity of cultural, intellectual and political life was great – perhaps feeling free to find its local expressions just because of a fundamentally shared philosophy of this world and the next.

Intellectual and Cultural Activity. Basic to mediaeval thought were the Bible, the tradition of the Church, which was above all embraced in the writings of the 'Fathers of the Church' although not confined to them, and the learning of Classical Greece and Rome. Insatiably active, students at all levels went to whoever had something to teach them: Muslim Arab scholars who preserved and studied ancient Greek writings, most importantly those of Aristotle; Jewish scholars, especially in Poland and Spain, who could enlighten them on the Hebrew of the Old Testament. Much further afield were the truly remarkable eastern journeys of the Polo family of Venice, and in particular Marco Polo's sojourn at the court of Kublai Khan. Real, if temporary, cultural and religious relations were established between Rome and Peking.

Reading, Writing and Making. People who have lost touch with Catholic tradition often find it hard to grasp the concept of a church teaching with authority, which yet encourages rather than inhibits ideas. Equally strange for many people in the modern west is a civilization in which reading and writing is treated as a special craft, alongside all the other special crafts in which men and women are skilled.

It is no accident that in the universities of the Middle Ages the student became a master of his subject, in the same way as in the multiplicity of arts, crafts and trades a person of sufficient knowledge and experience became a master of the 'mystery'. Mastership signified that a person was entrusted to teach; maturity therefore, as well as knowledge, was involved. As for 'mystery', this of course is not a complimentary name for a muddle. It reveals itself to its disciples in order that its truth may be served; it cannot be dictated to as if man were its creator in the first place. Here is the whole difference between the approach to life of wisdom and nature, and that of a technology which cannot think beyond the manipulation of matter.

Rich Civilization. Smallness in size was combined with international contacts. The population of the British Isles amounted to a few millions, for example (there are as many Catholics in England today as there were in the thirteenth century). There was not yet the psychological enclosure of the nation-state, and people were inveterate travellers – in about as much danger from highway robbers as today from motor accidents, that is to say, considerable but largely disregarded.

This both helped to produce, and in turn was influenced by, a distinct form of civilization. The pattern was not one of relatively small specialized groups and a mass of proletariate, called 'democratic' because each adult has a political vote, though little power over his own life and circumstances. Rather, it was that of the family extended throughout all forms of society; the network of guilds, for example social or for craft, music, painting, touching almost every activity; different forms of knighthood, including those providing service to the traveller and the sick; the vastly varied communities of what may be generally termed monks, friars and nuns; even hermits who were men and women not necessarily physically isolated, their little prayer-dwelling often being at some place of vital importance to the community, such as a bridge or river crossing.

The result of such social forms was a particular kind of culture arising from the very active contributions made by men and women out of their individual talents. It is one which perhaps bewilders people of modern times, who are more used to varying beliefs and moralities within general uniformity of exterior life, rather than unity of belief and morality, basically unchangeable, within marked diversity of life.

In Cornwall

Although no adequate study of mediaeval Cornwall has yet been made, the following comments will relate to what has just been said, and provide a setting for the studies in Part III.

We have to try to envisage a concentration of activities based on unity and diversity, the local and international. In this, religion (i.e. Christianity) was not a matter of personal taste nor the special province of the 'pious', let alone the outwardly respectable. It was the life-blood of the community.

It provided, therefore, a major source of interest and, it is not too much to say, of entertainment. What people find today in 'going shopping' – the colour, the variety, the very size and complexity of the buildings in which they are welcomed to wander at will, and in the life of which they participate according to their means and inclination, and from which they gain something to be their own; what they found in the estates of the post-sixteenth century squires – a sense of belonging to something greater than themselves, often dignified and beautiful, and in which each had his own recognized part to play, however small: all this and more is what church life meant, socially and materially, to mediaeval people. One difference to bear in mind in thinking of the small Cornish communities is that less was done *for* them and more was done *by* them than we can easily imagine in an age obsessed with 'ordinary people', which nevertheless treats them as lacking in rational, imaginative and even physically creative powers.

Popular Latin

Hard for us to imagine, too, is a way of life in which Latin is not a special study for an educated middle class, still less one subject out of many in which a school exam. may be taken, but simply a second language, learned to some degree by everyone who went beyond the 'ABC and Singing' of the little local school. It was spoken as a matter of course in centres of higher learning; as such, and as the official language of public worship, it formed an invaluable international tongue.

Those trying to picture the worship of those times, in and outside our Cornish churches, have sometimes frustrated their own efforts by overlooking the intensity of the local life, and also the general experience of Catholics until a very few years ago. The choir for sung Mass and Vespers would be made up of local men and boys of no necessary academic achievements, some picking up Latin on the way and learning and singing themselves into the language; as many members of choirs do today, though they have fewer advantages. The Latin Bible passages would be formally sung to their proper tones, but read to the congregations and expatiated upon in the local language – as has always happened. At Mass, the Lord's Prayer would be said or sung in Latin, familiar to everyone through constant repetition. But everyone would be familiar also with the Our Father, a form of the Hail Mary, and other prayers and hymns in their own tongue. These would be used not only in 'private' prayer but in popular devotions, which are no part of the Offices of formal worship, in and outside of the church on pilgrimages, for example. The existence of Latin, just because it belongs to no single nation-state, was, and remains, a protector of local languages. The most striking example of this in Cornish history occurs in the 'Prayer Book Rebellion' of 1549, a genuinely popular movement demanding not only the retention of the Mass as such, but at the same time of Latin and Cornish in face of the imposition of wholly English church services.

8. Lopérec in Brittany brings together angels and saints, and above the sacrificial Lamb, Celtic cross and Chi/Rho, with the alpha and omega of the Greek alphabet signifying that God is all in all.

The Living Bible

The Sacred Scriptures, with commentaries thereon, were the first study of scholars; parts were popularly very well known. These included passages related to various saints, but the Gospels above all, and those parts of the Old Testament most clearly looking forward to the Saviour – the Creation and the Fall of Man for instance, certain prophecies, Abraham and Isaac, the story of Jonah referred to by Christ himself as a sign of his death and resurrection, Noah and the Ark. We can still see this latter pictured in the late mediaeval glass of St Neot church, a tiny reminder of the colourful aspect of the churches in those times: stained glass, murals, painted stone carvings. Blisland church and the Catholic church at Launceston give us some impression of how things were, though not of the colour and variety in the dress of the worshippers. No longer are we customarily known by our habit, its design and colour.

Plays and Books – Glasney College

Belonging to the communities were the miracle or mystery plays, setting forth divine wonders and divine revelation. The plots might celebrate the local saint, Celtic, Biblical or other; but there were also the majestic series showing forth God's work and his dealings with mankind from the Creation to the End of the World. These, in the vernacular, are shot through with Biblical quotations and allusions. Many in Cornish were composed at Glasney College at Penryn, where the church was conducted on the popular pattern of canons living in community. It was a great centre of learning, but unlike Oxford, which had been pleased to send scholars to take up offices there, it did not survive the sixteenth century.

Also lost are nearly all the mediaeval (let alone earlier) hand-written and illustrated books. Cornwall was in a particularly unfortunate position because, on top of the fashionable contempt for manuscripts brought about by the arrival of printing and the massive destruction of such things as monastic libraries through religious hostility, came an increasingly strong suppression of things Cornish by English influences. Among the survivals are the Bodmin Gospels, a manuscript of an early date about 1000 AD, certain Lives of the Saints and, in Cornish, a few of the plays and a narrative poem on The Passion of Our Lord.

Living Structures

It may seem tedious to continue to remark that 'we must try to imagine . . .' but it is so easy to read not only our own times into past times but also our own uses of words. A comment is needed on the organization of church and social life. It is, for instance, misleading for us to think in terms of present day, or indeed post-sixteenth century, lords and tenants. It might be said that in mediaeval times *no one* belonged solely to himself, and the group or 'family' to which a person belonged was inter-related with others. In such things there would be an interacting structure of rights and duties, underlined by those written legal records of which mediaeval society was so fond. Thus when we hear, among numerous instances, that the church of Lanlivery belonged to the Manor of Bodardle and was given, with its chapelries of Lostwithiel and Luxulyan, to the Priory of Tywardreath in about 1150, it must not be thought that 'possession' implied that Bodardle Manor or the Benedictine monks at Tywardreath could do just what they pleased with the people or buildings involved. Tywardreath Priory itself looked to the Abbey of Angers, on the border of Brittany and Anjou, from which it had been founded, and ran into difficulties when that link was broken. Thus this kind of structural relationship not only frequently went beyond the bounds of the locality, but could be international. The growing towns — though always very small by modern standards — gradually formed more independent bodies, but always their lives were shaped by custom, regulations, and the protective powers of interlocking groups. Lostwithiel's Charter of 1189, to take one of many instances, while establishing certain freedoms and rights, was the very reverse of a licence for a free-for-all.

SIXTEENTH CENTURY TO
MODERN TIMES

Discussion of the events of the mid and later sixteenth century is inevitably endless. As in the tenth century, which heralded one of the most violent breaches between east and west Christian communities, there had been intellectual disorder, political and social upheavals, and a crying need for Church reform. Fundamental discussion for Christians centres on the question: which was reform and which was change so radical as to be called, without intended offence, revolution?

The first major feature in the new landscape is the Church of England, established by law and until fairly recently supported by legal sanctions against those who refused to accept a national church. It moulded much of English life, and strongly affected Cornwall. At the same time, this predominance must not be allowed to obscure the existence, multiplication, and contributions of non-conformist bodies, whether earlier ones such as Baptists and the Society of Friends, or later, such as — and in Cornwall above all — the Methodist Church, including Bible Christians. Over the centuries, Catholics, against whom the most repressive of the laws were directed, were reduced in Cornwall to a few hundreds; growth began again when restrictions on normal social and professional, as well as religious, life were lifted early in the nineteenth century.

All this produced a new situation concerning the personal veneration and public honouring of 'saints'. This is examined in a historical setting in Part IV.

WHAT MAKES A SAINT?

Reading about the ever-varied individuals for whom the Church has authorized the use of the title, Saint, is the best introduction to the nature of sanctity. The following notes and definitions may clear up some points which are often not well understood.

Saint. The word is derived from the Latin *Sanctus,* meaning holy, consecrated (in Greek ʻαγιος ; hence *hagiography*, the study of the saints). It is significant, too, that 'holy' itself comes from the Old English *hal* meaning whole, healthy. You are not less of a person the more that evil is expelled from your system!

Saint Christopher was an early Christian martyr. About him there grew the story of how he wished to serve the mightiest masters, human or satanic, and how he learned in the end to carry the light weight of the Christ-Child, which is yet

9. Saint Christopher; one of two mediaeval wall paintings at Poughill.

heavy with all the needs of the world, and in whose apparent helplessness lies the only real power, at the heart of the world. This most popular of saints is also a symbol of all saints. His name itself means Christ-bearer, a name applied to their vocation by early Christians. It is in this sense, familiar in the Bible, that all Christians are called to be saints: Christ-bearers in this world and sharers in His glory in the next.

Martyrs. The word is from the Greek, the common language of the earliest Christians: μαρτυς, a witness. With Saints Peter and Paul and the other apostles, foundations of the living Church and, in any case, all martyrs save John the Evangelist, the martyrs were the first saints in the more precise sense. By the offering of their lives in witness to the truth of Christ, they became intimately associated with the sacrifice of Calvary, and through their incorporation in the resurrected Lord in heavenly glory became themselves 'mediators' of grace to the world.

Altar-Tombs. In recognition of the foregoing, the Sacrifice of the Lord's Supper was whenever possible offered over the treasured remains of a martyr. By this rite, named Eucharist, or simply the Liturgy, in Greek, and Mass in Latin, the community is intimately present at the eternal offering of Jesus to the Father, and its members are made one with him by receiving that offered Body and Blood. When the Church was freed from legal restrictions in the Roman Empire, church buildings were erected and adorned, and the altar-tombs embellished. (See Endelienta in Part II.)

House-Churches. In early Christian Rome, and elsewhere, people naturally met in each other's houses for Christian assemblies and worship. Sometimes a house used in this way became the site of a Church; St Cecilia's in the Trastevere district of Rome is an outstanding example. The young lady, later to be acclaimed patron saint of music, was martyred in the home which she had made a centre of Christian life. Her body was buried in one of the catacombs, but in later times of freedom brought back and enshrined under the high altar of the church erected where her home had stood. This lovely church has received much in the way of new building and embellishment in later periods. We may be at once reminded of many churches in Cornwall where the original foundation was the home and chapel of an individual devoted to the service of God and the spreading of the Gospel. (See Part II, under Buryan, for instance.)

Shrines. From such things grew all the rich elaboration of later times. There are still altars which have been placed over the whole body of a saint (not necessarily a martyr), but, more commonly, a small relic, a part of a saint's body, is enshrined in an altar. As time went on, various altars in churches were dedicated to a great variety of these friends in Heaven. Shrines can also treasure such relics as a part of a saint's clothing, or simply a much-loved and grace-bearing picture or statue, which may be called in general terms an icon.

'Christian Materialism'. For those for whom so physical an interpretation of the Christian life is unfamiliar, it may briefly be noted that it springs from the natural in mankind (fulfilled not denied by Christianity) and a profound meditation on the belief that 'the Word was made Flesh' – and remains so. The vigorously Biblical tradition of fasting with prayer bears witness to the importance of the human body: as with mind, heart and soul, it too must be 'emptied' to receive God. Creation as such is good and holy: the Devil, by definition, cannot create, either matter or spirit. What corrupts and disrupts is sin, and thus comes death: the withdrawal of the human soul and the disintegration of the body. But as Saint Gregory of Tours (among many others) has said of the sinless Mother of Jesus: 'The Lord took Mary's holy body and conveyed it on a cloud to Paradise; there it was again united with her soul . . . ' In Heaven, all the Blessed rejoice in the presence of God, and of each other in the Communion of Saints, which extends its fellowship to the faithful on earth. But even this is in a sense imperfect until the fullness of time brings the resurrection of the body and the completion of the human person (see of course notably the writings of Saint Paul).

10. The altar-tomb of St Endelienta, as it has survived in St Endellion church.

Canonization. Essentially, the saint – the intercessor in Heaven, is 'guaranteed' as such by Church authority. The contemporary Catholic form of canonization grew up over many centuries: the rigorous examination of the life and of miracles claimed to have followed prayer by, or to, the person; the proclamation and accompanying festivities at St Peter's in Rome and in the places where the requests for the canonization had originated. In earlier times, that element in the Church's life named tradition was enough; Saint Peter was never formally canonized any more than was Saint Petroc. The vast spread and proliferation of Christian life, and the speedy growth of something rather different from classic

tradition, that is, popular traditions, made definite organization necessary. The
popular in one shape or another is still essential. Perhaps the most striking
example of such acclaim followed the murder of Thomas Becket in Canterbury
Cathedral. His fame as saint and martyr spread through Christendom from
Iceland to Armenia with such speed that the canonization process was begun
almost at once; and it being successful, he was proclaimed saint only three years
after his death.

Patron Saints

As in the custom of taking a saint's name at Confirmation in the Catholic
Church, any person, any group, any place, can take a saint for patron. Attempts
are made from Rome, from time to time, to sort out confusions which can arise
in this most common and world-wide habit, partly by exhortation, partly by
setting up lists for the registration of patron saints.

This may helpfully shed light on the vexed question: who is Cornwall's patron
saint? Basically, it is a question of whom the Cornish people themselves wish to
choose, but also in what way they wish to choose – for what reason is a patron
saint wanted, and to what degree do they wish the choice to be formally
recognized.

Problems of varying popular traditions can be resolved. Merely for example:
the Archangel Saint Michael (see Part III) could be recognized as patron of the
land of Cornwall, the country of Kernow; while Saint Piran (see Part II) could
be called upon as patron of the Cornish people. The apparent neglect of Saint
Petroc or, if I may say so, of a woman, in such a choice, would be no more real
than it is in the fact that Saint David is patron of Wales, although Saint Illtud was
equally important historically.

Feast

One of the delightful aspects of Cornish life is the genuine survival of the Feast:
the celebration of the patron of the parish church and the locality, despite the
destruction of formal veneration in the sixteenth century, the onslaught of
seventeenth century puritanism, and that element of eighteenth and nineteenth
century Methodism and Evangelicalism which was bitterly hostile to things
supposedly peculiarly 'Roman Catholic'. More than, say, Chapel Anniversary,
more than the usual Patronal Festival of the Anglican Church, more than most
Catholic festivals as commonly now celebrated in Great Britain, the Cornish
Feast maintains the fullest tradition, in which church and chapel and community
round about join instinctively, without that self-consciousness over 'sacred' and
'secular' which has been the curse of a divided Christendom.

Dictionary lovers will find this illustrated in the Cornish word *gol* signifying
parish feast, festival, holiday, revel, banquet, and also watch and vigil. This latter
reminds us that the Christian day, following ancient custom, starts before
midnight. Thus the eve or vigil is the beginning of – the entering into – the feast.

FEAST DAYS & CALENDARS,
SAINTS & HOLY PEOPLE

Feasts and Calendars

The 1969 edition of the official Roman Calendar remarks in its dignified and universal Latin *Calendarium natura sua est mutabile* . . . 'By their very nature calendars are subject to change . . . ' The passage goes on to refer to the necessity of finding places for the feast days of new saints.

The situation over Feast Days is, however, a good deal more complicated than this. The Roman Calendar deals mainly with those saints whose festivals are to be kept by the Catholic churches throughout the world – a minority of highly distinguished men and women. There are only 365 days in the year and not on all of these – most Sundays for instance, and Holy Week – can a saint be celebrated.

There are, then, lesser Calendars, those for example which include patron saints of individual countries who may not have marked world-wide significance. Different dioceses, Church of England as well as Catholic, will celebrate certain saints historically associated with their own neighbourhood. Moreover, many religious orders honour saints of their own whose lives are especially meaningful to them (in September alone the Canons Regular of the Lateran, whose Cornish house was Bodmin Abbey, celebrate eight saints and martyrs, ranging in date from the eighth century to the French Revolution).

The fundamental Calendar historically, and the origin of formal lives of the saints, is the Roman Martyrology. As its name suggests, this began as lists of the commemorations of the martyrs under the persecutions of the Roman Empire. Each was, if possible, celebrated on his or her 'birthday', that is the day of death and of birth into eternal life, when an account of the saint's life, and in particular of the circumstances of the martyrdom, was read out.

The complications by the time we reach mediaeval times can be imagined, with the vast proliferation of saints, many of international fame, and the intense local life, lives and legends of favourite saints, and highly localized calendars.

For this reason, as well as the loss of many written records and stable traditions over the later centuries, the identification of feast days for the Celtic saints is not always easy. Sometimes no date has survived at all. Sometimes different sources give different dates, and not only for Celtic saints. Firmly established and recognized feast days, such as those of Saint Piran and Saint Petroc, may well mark the day of death – the custom which has been generally followed for all saints; tradition carried from former times into the Middle Ages was very strong.

With church dedications of mediaeval and later times, the situation is much more straightforward. Very occasional variations can be found between the Anglican Book of Common Prayer and Roman dates, especially through recent changes in the Roman Calendar, which appear also in the Church of England Common Worship Calendar.

The Orthodox Church, and others of the east, have numerous calendars of their own, to which some saints have been added in the centuries following the clear division from Roman authority. The most widely used, among Churches in communion with Rome as well as others, is the Byzantine Calendar. There is a certain amount of agreement between eastern and western traditions over the dates of major and ancient feast days.

Good People and Symbolic Figures

All human traditions bear witness to the need for heroes and heroines, of one sort or another, who become something more to the community than simply people with interesting or even significant histories. This book deals with saints in the Catholic and Celtic traditions, which combine at depth the personal and the communal: great goodness, which is a bridge between earth and Heaven, embodied in a man or woman around whose head shines splendour.

This of course implies no denigration of other good people. The Feast of All Saints which starts, or should start, on Hallowe'en (the Eve of All Hallows – All Saints) celebrates everyone in Heaven. Not to be neglected are those who are remembered with special honour, and have become in varying ways symbolic and charismatic figures. For Cornwall there have been, for instance, Loveday Hambly, the Wesley Brothers, Billy Bray, Robert Stephen Hawker, not to speak of King Charles I. (See Part IV).

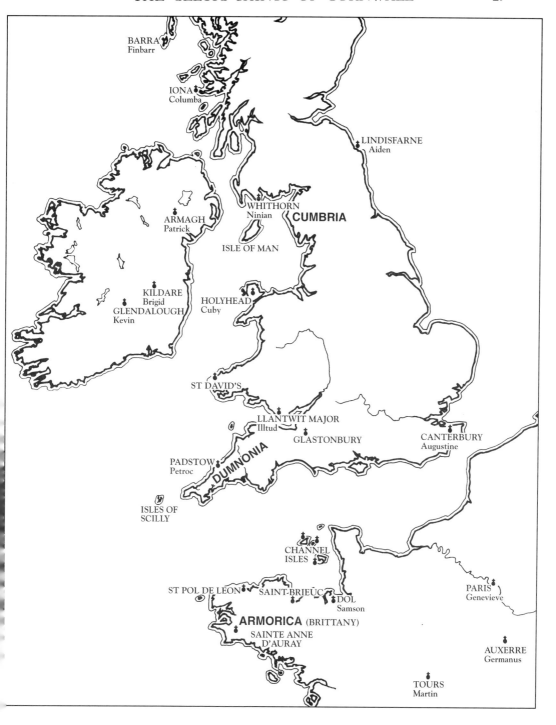

11. Some Celtic Christian centres, fourth to early seventh centuries.

Key

1. Cuby - Holyhead
2. Petroc - Verwig
3. Breoc - St Briavels
4. Piran - Cardiff
5. Petroc - St Petrox
6. Cadoc - Llangattock
7. Keyne - Llangenny
8. Samson - Llantwit Major
9. Petroc - Timberscombe
10. Petroc - Petrockstow
11. Petroc - Bodmin
12. Kea - Landkey
13. David - Davidstow
14. Cadoc - Harlyn Bay
15. St Breock
16. Piran - Perranzabuloe
17. Meryadoc - Camborne
18. Gwinear
19. Samson - Scilly Isles
20. Paul Aurelian - Paul
21. Melaine - Mullion
22. Winwaloe - Landewednack
23. St Kea
24. St Mewan
25. Fimbarrus - Fowey
26. St Winnow
27. Cuby - Duloe
28. St Keyne
29. Samson - South Hill
30. Petroc - Dartmouth
31. Gwinear - Pluvigner
32. Meryadoc - Pontivy
33. Petroc - Lopérec
34. Winwaloe - Landévennec
35. Kea - Cleder
36. Paul Aurelian - St Pol de Léon
37. Piran - Trézélidé
38. Mewan - Saint-Méen
39. Samson - Dol
40. Samson - Guernsey
41. Saint-Brieuc
42. Melaine - Rennes
43. Winnow - Bergues-Saint-Winnoc

12. Some widespread dedications of Celtic saints.

PART II

The Celtic Saints of Cornwall

Prayer of Saint Meryadoc

Arluth, a wruk mor ha tyr,
    pup ur-oll re'm weresso,
Ha roy dhym y'n forth a wyr
    ow bewnans omma gedya.
Yesu, Arluth, orthyf myr,
    ha'th lel gras dhymmo grontya:
Yesu, pup ur-oll ow desyr
    yu y'n bys-ma dha blesya.

Lord, who made sea and land,
    always give me aid,
And guide my life here
    in the way of truth.
Lord Jesu, look on me,
    and grant me thy unfailing grace.
Every hour, Jesu, it is my desire
    in this world to please you.

(From *Bewnans Meryasek*)

THE CELTIC SAINTS
OF CORNWALL

This alphabetical section does not attempt to list every possible name of a presumed saint surviving in a place-name, nor to identify a Celtic patron for every church in Cornwall. The vast majority will be found here; if there is no entry, then it has reluctantly been decided that there is nothing helpful to be said. A parish or place which may feel itself thus orphaned is reminded that the adoption of a second, or indeed a wholly new, patron need not be regarded as an eccentric proceeding. It is, in fact, much more 'traditional' for the people living in a given period to honour a patron who is meaningful to them than to commemorate a name simply because it might have been the 'original'. Christianity is based essentially on history; but it is not a slave of the past.

Considering the variety of names – British or Celtic, from Roman civilization, Latinized forms through Christian usage, the effects of speech, of various spellings in writing, and the simple passage of time, we are very fortunate to have so many generally accepted forms. It has not been possible to list every name exactly as it may exist in a place-name. It is hoped that the occasional cross-references will enable the reader to find any which do not bear close resemblance to what appears on the maps or which need clarification for other reasons. Feast dates are given where possible.

ADWEN. Advent near Camelford does not take its name from the season of the Church's year, as might be thought, but from Adwen, named as one of the daughters of King Brychan. According to certain traditions, this famous local king who gave his name to Brycheiniog (Breconshire, south Wales) was the father of numerous children – twenty-four is the most favoured number, all of whom became church founders, some in Wales, some in Devon, some in Cornwall. As with Adwen herself, we often have no historical information about them beyond the dedication of the church and the name of the place. The appearance of the saints' names in lists of the Children of Brychan is not until much later than the original foundations. The work, however, of these men and women can be seen in the very number of places to which they left their names; and the story of the children of King Brychan and Queen Gladwisa may at least remind us that many accounts of saints in Celtic lands tell us of both families and friends working in co-operation.

Adwen herself is credited in legend with being the very benevolent patron of sweethearts. Happy thoughts about the replacement of Saint Valentine by this young woman in Cornish popular custom may at first be dashed when we learn that a date for a Feast of Saint Adwen has not survived. However this very fact means that February 14th is as good a date as any other, though perhaps the parish of Advent should be consulted first.

ALLEN. Alan - to use the form which is best known – is a Celtic name, and is popular in Brittany as well, of course, as in the north of England and Scotland. There was a Welsh saint of this name who became Bishop of the important and graceful town of Quimper in Brittany, and it seems likely that it was he who gave the name to St Allen, north of Truro.

ANTA appears to have given her name to Lelant – Lananta (a glance at the location on the towans above the Hayle estuary shows the impossibility of the interpretation of 'religious house in the valley'). She was not necessarily the original founder of what became the parish church (see Uny); the site of her own little house and chapel was probably commemorated by the nearby mediaeval chapel of Saint Anta. This in turn is commemorated for us by the place-name on the point, Chapel Anjou, a location which makes probable, as well as picturesque, the existence of Saint Anta's Light at the mouth of the estuary.

AUSTELL. There is a mediaeval Breton Life of the popular Saint Mewan which says that he was godfather to Austell, or Austol, when the latter was baptized into the Christian Church. In due course, Austell was also ordained to the priesthood, and the two friends lived for a while in the same monastery in Brittany. They were companions of the great Saint Samson in his work in Brittany and Cornwall, and were founders of the two parishes, next door to each other, of Saint Mewan and Saint Austell. (The latter church received an additional mediaeval dedication to the Holy Trinity, as is illustrated by the very fine carvings on the west face of the tower.) Only very shortly did death part them for, as Mewan had foretold, he himself died first and within a week his friend Austell had followed him to Heaven. The tradition of the friendship of the two saints survived in St Austell for at least a time after the destruction of the mid-sixteenth century. Feast day: June 28th.

BREACA. It would seem that the patron of Breage was one of a group of missionaries from Ireland, of whom another was her friend Crowan, and a third was Germoe. The little estuary of the Hayle River (*hayl* means estuary) provided an inviting landing-place on the inhospitable north coast, though human hospitality might be conspicuously lacking. However, Breaca and her companions escaped the violence of King Teudrig – see Gwinear.

BREOC was born in Dyfed (Cardiganshire, west Wales), and an account tells that, following an angel's instruction to his good-living pagan parents, the boy was sent for Christian education to Saint Germanus (see his entry). The two are associated in the eastern French and Belgian area, where boys are still named Brieuc. In due course, the young man was ordained priest and returned to his own country where he converted his parents to Christianity. With 168 friends and disciples he travelled to Brittany, no doubt crossing Cornwall by the 'Saints Way' route, on which he has left his name at St Breock, near Wadebridge. From the great Breton monastery that he founded grew up the important town, with an impressive cathedral, of Saint-Brieuc. Feast day: May 1st.

BREVITA. There is a tenacious claim at Lanlivery, now an upland hamlet but in mediaeval times an important centre, that the patron saint is Brevita or, in less Latinized form, Bryvyth. There is possible support for this at Lanlivry in Brittany. A Celtic founder is of course very likely; though it is perhaps strange that in this area the traces of a Celtic dedication at Luxulyan also should be so confused, and at Lostwithiel, among others, non-existent. Of other suggestions

13. The patron of Breage, pictured with emblems of her voyage from Ireland and her church
foundation, within the wreath of eternal glory.

for Lanlivery, very attractive is a later one of Saint Dunstan (see Part III).

BREWARD. This patron of a village and church on the western heights of Bodmin Moor is an example of how these saints journeyed from place to place. He has left forms of his name, of which Branwalder is probably closest to the original, not only in Brittany in the form of Broladre, but also in Jersey – St Brelade. He was a companion, at least for a time, of Saint Samson, whose work was so important to Cornwall and still more to Brittany, and who himself visited the Channel Isles. Feast day: February 9th.

BUDOC. This is the saint of Budock the mother church of Falmouth, and of St Budeaux, once a village but now one of the constituent parts of the conglomeration of Plymouth. His name is also found in Brittany, and there, as in Cornwall, it is geographically close to that of Saint Mawes, a combination which suggests they were friends and companions in their labours. A Life of Saint Budoc has survived, of the kind which contains good stories not intended to be taken too literally. This tells us that Budoc was of Breton origin, for family enemies placed his mother in a great cask at Brest and committed her to the mercy of the sea. Therein she gave birth to her son Budoc, and after many months they came to shore on the coast of Ireland. There is also, however, an interesting historical element in the account of Saint Budoc as Bishop of Dol. This great foundation made by Saint Samson had for its second bishop Samson's cousin Saint Magloire, and the cathedral is dedicated to them both. When Magloire retired to a life of solitude, Budoc became the new bishop. But he was unable to keep Magloire nearby, as he had hoped, for a call came from the Channel Islands which had already been visited by Samson. The monastery which Magloire founded on Sark was central to the life of the Channel Islands for centuries. Feast day: December 8th.

BURYAN. This is the form which is found in the place-name of West Penwith, but we also meet Berriona, Beriana, Beryan; the last seems, for various reasons, the most convincing. The early mediaeval Exeter Calendar or Martyrology, listing saints to be honoured in the diocese, describes her as an Irish maiden through whose prayers a son of King Gerent was cured of paralysis (for this Cornish family, see Gerent and Selevan). The place is an interesting religious centre, as it is one of those where the great early English king, Athelstan, established a somewhat different style religious house from the Celtic monastery which had already grown up there. This was a college of canons, that is, a community of priests living, studying and working together – a form of life very popular in mediaeval times (see Part I). The grandeur of the fifteenth century church gives some idea of what its earlier dignity must have been, and other holy people, such as the Blessed Virgin Mary, Saint Andrew and Saint Nicholas, became associated in the dedication. But the young Irish maiden was always regarded as the foundress, from whose small hermitage, dwelling and chapel, all took its rise. Feast day: May 1st.

Veryan, in one of the loveliest areas of Cornwall, between Veryan Bay and Gerrans Bay, may take its name from the saint of Buryan; Gerrans takes its name from Saint Gerent. But it has also been suggested that the place-name is due to a shortening of Symphorian, patron of its church (see this saint in Part III).

CADOC. There is no parish church dedication to this famous Welsh saint in Cornwall, but a centre of devotion was his chapel and holy well in the parish of Padstow, near the shore of Harlyn Bay. He is one of the foremost saints of Wales, founder of a great monastery at Llancarfan in Powys (Glamorgan) where many Celtic saints received their religious formation, including the famous Saint Brendan of Ireland and Saint Malo of Brittany. In addition to connections with Saint Mawgan, he is said in Welsh tradition to have been a nephew of Petroc (patron, of course, of Padstow) and also to have gone on pilgrimage to Saint Michael's Mount, where he met his aunt Saint Keyne. There are many church dedications to Cadoc in the South Wales border country, some with nearby dedications to Saint Keyne, as at Llangattock and Llangenny between Abergavenny and Brecon, the neighbourhood to which he retired to die. He is also remembered in Brittany and Scotland. Feast day: September 25th.

CLEER. Presumably there was an earlier church and community founder, perhaps with a similar name, at the windswept St Cleer on the southern edge of Bodmin Moor. The Cleer now commemorated there was Clarus, an Englishman of the eighth-ninth century, who became a monk in Normandy; but he can conveniently be included here. His story is somewhat sensational, though in human experience by no means impossible. A monastery is of course an intrinsic part of the community, having many contacts with people living around about. Cleer was pestered by the attentions of a local noblewoman, who felt that her passions and her rank could over-ride his monastic vows and indeed his own wishes. He fled to an isolated hermitage but his persecutor, in a rage of spite, had him pursued and murdered. This was at the place which thus came to be known as Saint-Claire-sur-Epte, and his fame spread quite widely.

The dedication of this handsome Cornish church with its interesting mediaeval history, when it belonged for three hundred years to the Knights Hospitallers, has nothing therefore to do with Saint Clare of Assisi, friend of Saint Francis and founder of the Poor Clares. In the town there is also to be seen St Cleer's holy well within a fine fifteenth century building. Feast day: November 4th.

CLETHER's name is in the surviving Cornish list of the Children of Brychan (see Adwen), otherwise we have no written information about this saint. However, the hamlet of St Clether, north of Altarnun, is well worth a visit, not only for the charmingly situated mediaeval parish church and eighteenth century vicarage, but for the ancient chapel and well of St Clether. These stand about half a mile up the little valley of the Inny, and they have been put in order so that much of the pattern of early days can be appreciated and enjoyed in the country setting, even if colour and imagery could add a little more still. Feast day: November 4th.

COAN. This is the saint of Merther, between Tresillian and St Michael Penkevil on the east bank of the river Fal. The small building there was only briefly a parish church, but a chapel and well of Saint Coan formerly existed. The name of the place, however, gives one important piece of information about the saint: the Cornish *merther* means martyr, so Coan was martyred, and very likely on this spot – the place of the death was usually cherished. The Celtic saints might sometimes be working among unfriendly people, but these were not often militantly hostile, and Coan may be especially honoured as one who witnessed to the Faith of Christ in the shedding of his blood.

COLAN. All we know of the patron of pleasant little Colan, off the St Columb Major – St Columb Minor road, is a connection with Wales and Brittany hardly unusual in the saints of Cornwall, and possibly Glastonbury (see Kea). His name is found in Llangollen, Clwyd (north Wales) now internationally famous for its festival, and in Langolen in Brittany. A late mediaeval Life of the saint has survived in Welsh. But this is of the sort which does not so much set out to present a historical account as to give exciting stories and moral lessons, and similar ones are often used to sing the praises of different saints. Feast day: May 20th.

14. The chapel and well of Saint Clether.

COLUMB. Columba is Latin for dove. It is not surprising that this great Biblical symbol of peace and salvation and, in particular, of the Holy Spirit, should have given us a common Christian name. Of the saints, men and women who have borne the name, best known are the two sixth-seventh century Irishmen: Columba, apostle of Scotland, and Columban, missionary to the European continent. Nicholas Roscarrock, writing in the late sixteenth century (see under Endelienta), records the tradition that the name-saint of the picturesque St Columb Major, and little St Columb Minor now virtually part of Newquay, was a Christian maiden who refused the attentions of a pagan suitor. She fled his anger but he came in pursuit, and when she refused his demand that she renounce her Faith, he beheaded her. This was said to have taken place at Ruthvos in St Columb Major parish, where there is a spring of water commemorating the virgin martyr. The place-name certainly suggests a long memory of some such occurrence, *ruth* being Cornish for red, while *vos* is possibly *fos* – wall. The actual spot where the blood of the martyr is shed becomes a holy, and therefore long remembered, place. That this type of story is told of other Christian maidens (Agatha in Sicily and Winifred in Wales, for example) does not mean it is not basically factual, though fictional details grow up over the centuries. It is a kind of situation which must have quite often arisen with Christian young girls living in a largely pagan society, where the free choice of marriage – and still more of dedicated virginity – was not fully understood, and antagonism towards Christianity added to the fury of pride and passion.

CONAN. There are two possible choices for the patron of the little church at Washaway, founded from Egloshayle. There was a Conan who was associated with Saint Petroc, and this of course is in the heart of Petroc's land. There was also the distinguished Cornishman chosen to be the first bishop of King Athelstan's foundation at St Germans (see Part I). Feast day: this is observed on July 23rd, the date of the dedication of the present building in 1881.

CONGAR. There is no parish under the patronage of this saint in Cornwall, but there was a chapel at Lanivet, near Bodmin, and the name has survived in a farm named St Ingonger. He was connected with the very important Cadoc and Petroc, but is particularly interesting because of the veneration given to him in Somerset, as well as in the more to be expected Wales and Brittany. An imaginative Life was written of him at Wells in the early Middle Ages, which bears witness to his popularity. It is a reminder that we should not restrict the term 'Celtic' to modern frontiers (see Part I), nor regard the life of the Church as being divided into hard and fast areas. Feast day: May 20th.

CONSTANTINE. This name is associated with two very attractive and very different parts of Cornwall – the parish just above a creek of the Helford River, and Constantine Bay with the remains of a chapel and a holy well among the golf links near Padstow. The most famous Constantine is the fourth century Roman emperor who was mainly responsible for making Christianity a legally recognized religion in the Empire, and after whom was named Constantinople, capital of the Empire in the East and one of the great cities of the world. It is not, therefore, a surprising name to find, whether as a Roman survival or as one honoured among Christians. Appropriately, Saint Constantine himself was a 'king' – one of the simple rulers of small areas who are to be found before countries and people become very sophisticated, in early Wales and Ireland too, for example, and in the way of life depicted by Homer where a princess does the family washing. According to a Scottish account, Constantine gave up his throne to his son after the death of his wife. He became a simple monk in Ireland, where his identity was only discovered when he was overheard laughing contentedly and saying 'King Constantine of Cornwall – here he is working at a mill!' This account also links him, later, with the work of Saint Columba in Scotland, and he is said to have been Scotland's first martyr. As the saintly King of the Cornish he came to be famous and venerated also in Wales, although such was the popularity of the name Constantine that records take a good deal of disentangling. He may be for instance the Constantine converted by Saint Petroc (see the latter's entry). Feast day (in Cornwall): March 9th.

CRANTOCK. A Latin life of Saint Crantock, or Carantoc, written in Wales, tells among other things of how King Arthur asked him to rid the land of a marauding dragon: 'Then the blessed Carantoc prayed to the Lord, and immediately the dragon came running, making a loud noise; and it humbly bent

15. The banner of Saint Crantock at Carantec in Brittany.

its head before the servant of God, who put his stole round its neck and led it like a lamb, and it did not lift its wings or its claws'. It is gratifying to learn that after this the saint did not permit the warriors to kill the captive monster, but sent it off with instructions to behave itself in the future. This is an example of how tales of early saints and of King Arthur who, in his historical form, belongs to the same period, came to be intermingled from time to time. More factually, it is possible that he was a son of Ceredig, who gave his name to Cardigan, and that he was a helper of Saint Patrick in Ireland. Like a number of Celtic saints he was venerated in Somerset as also, of course, at Crantock across the River Gannel from Newquay in Cornwall, and Carantec in north Brittany. Feast day: May 16th.

CREED. The church of Creed, just south of Grampound, is named after a Saint Crida of whom little is known, except that from the form of her name presumably she was a woman. (See also Sancreed.) She may be the same person as Saint Grada on the Lizard; her name has also been associated with the foundation of Crediton in Celtic Devon.

CROWAN is said to have come to Cornwall with her friend Breaca; the two foundations, Crowan and Breage, are not far from each other. At the place named after her a round field still marks the *lan* (see Place Names 3, p. 141) within which was the chapel and dwelling. Saint Uny is also remembered here, and the parish Feast is in fact on his day (see his entry).

CUBERT is probably the Gwbert of the Cardigan neighbourhood of Dyfed in west Wales, which seems to have had especial connections with the area just south of Newquay (see Crantock, for example). Cubert has made his mark in Cornwall for, as well as the village that bears his name, his is the well of nearby Holywell Bay and its hamlet. In the fourteenth century, the dedication of the church became mixed up with the name of the celebrated Saint Cuthbert of Lindisfarne, the kind of thing that can easily happen if active memory fades and some similar name has become very well known.

CUBY (or Kebi as we see at Holyhead church) is rare among the Cornish saints in having being born in Cornwall of a Cornish family. His father is said to have been Saint Selevan (see his entry). Possibly he was born at Cuby near Tregony (his church there is now the parish church of Tregony), though claims are also made for Duloe, situated between the two branches of the Looe River, of whose church he is the original patron. Cuby followed the great missionary customs of the Celtic saints, but going in the opposite direction from the Irish and Welsh coming to Cornwall. From place-names, and to some extent the mediaeval Life of the Saint, we trace his journeyings, to Ireland and above all in Wales. He has been called 'one of the makers of Christian Wales'. His great centre was the monastery which he founded at what is known in English as Holyhead on Holy Island, the famous Anglesey port for Ireland, and, as a still more direct memorial, named in Welsh Caergybi. Feast day: November 8th.

CURY. Cury is a form of the name Corentin. In Cornwall his parish is on the Lizard, but his chief importance is in Brittany. He was the first bishop of the handsome and important town of Quimper, centre of the area known as Cornouaille. Corentin is one of the most famed of the Breton saints. His festival is a great celebration, his praises being sung and his patronage invoked in Breton, Latin and French. Indeed, until the French Revolution's attack on the Christian Church, the city was known as Quimper-Corentin. Feast day: December 12th.

16. The well of Saint Cuby, the greatest of the early saints of Cornish family; near Duloe.

DAVID, of course, has become the patron saint of Wales – Dewi Sant. He was the celebrated abbot-bishop (see Part I) of what is now Saint David's at Mynyw in far west Wales. (The Latin form of Mynyw, Menevia, is once again familiar as one of the Catholic dioceses of Wales today.) Irish saints in particular seem to have come to Mynyw to benefit from Saint David's character and teaching, and to take back to Ireland the inspiration of the austerely beautiful life of his monastery. He was very important in Welsh life, above all in the south and west; and he is also honoured in Brittany, and in Cornwall at Davidstow just north of Bodmin Moor. We do not know if he actually visited the area, though the dedication of Altarnun, only a few miles away, to his mother (see Saint Non) happily suggests some particular connection. As the Celtic saints were such great travellers, it is perhaps appropriate that a church dedication which honours him in Devon should be best known to hundreds of thousands of people as Exeter St David's Railway Station! Feast day: March 1st.

DAY. Nothing is known of this saint except that he may be a Saint Dei who is venerated in Brittany. The parish, in the rather dramatic country east of Redruth, was formed out of part of Gwennap in the nineteenth century. The area is, however, distinguished for two reasons. In mediaeval times, the chapel of the Holy Trinity at what was already named Saint Day was one of the greatest places of pilgrimage in Cornwall. The place has also given us an ancient Christmas carol, the Saint Day Carol (rather confusedly named Sans Day Carol in *The Oxford Book of Carols*). This has now become widely known, though hitherto apparently sung by the people of the district alone. It is of the same popular type as 'The Holly and the Ivy', but has a charm of its own:

> Now the Holly bears a berry
> as green as the grass:
> And Mary bore Jesus
> who died on the cross;
>
> And Mary bore Jesus Christ
> our Saviour for to be,
> And the first tree in the greenwood
> it was the Holly.

DENNIS. See Part III.

DOCCO. See Kew.

DOMINICK. See Part III.

ELWYN was apparently one of the saints who came over from Ireland with Breaca (see her entry) and it is his name which is linked to 'porth' – landing-place or harbour, in what is now Porthleven, close to Breage. There was a chapel there dedicated to him, but he had to wait very many centuries more for a parish church. In the nineteenth century through local genius in developing mining engineering and the steam engine, Hayle, on the north coast, developed into a small town of very considerable importance; and in 1870 Hayle parish was formed out of part of Phillack parish, with a newly built church named in memory of Saint Elwyn.

ENDELIENTA. The patron of St Endellion in the country near Port Isaac on the north coast of Cornwall. In this parish lived Nicholas Roscarrock, who included in his 'Catalogue of the Saints of Great Britain' valuable studies of what was then known in fact and folk history of many Cornish saints, just after the period when their veneration had been suppressed. His house is now the picturesque farm of Roscarrock. Nicholas was one of the lay people arrested with Saint Cuthbert Mayne at Golden Manor in 1577 (see Part IV).

Nicholas Roscarrock tells us that the altar-tomb of Saint Endelienta in the church 'was defaced in King Henrie the 8 time and afterwards placed upon one Mr Batten'. This provides a vivid reminder of the shrines, often containing bones of the saints, which existed in such churches, providing a more immediate link with the church founder than any written record. Thanks to Roscarrock, we have been able to identify the altar-tomb, and it is now preserved with due honour in the spacious and dignified church.

Roscarrock could find little in the way of written information about the saint – she appears as one of the Children of Brychan (see Adwen) and at St Endellion presumably she settled and taught the Christian faith. He writes with care and precision: 'There are two wells which bear her name in the parish, the one somewhat more distant from the church than the other which hath been as it seems found out of late for more convenience to serve the church; but that which is more remote is said to be frequented by her in her life time'. Her feast day is April 29th.

ENODOC. The church of Saint Enodoc on the right bank of the Camel Estuary provides as romantic an example of a building in a landscape as any in Cornwall. However, we know nothing of the early Saint to whom we owe it, except that in mediaeval times he was venerated at Bodmin Priory, which suggests that he had some especial connections with Bodmin or maybe was regarded as a person of some importance. He is not to be confused with the patron of St Enoder (not far from Summercourt) about whom we have no information at all, though a few more or less exotic suggestions have been made.

ERBYN. See under Ervan.

ERME. See Part III.

ERNEY. All that can be said of this saint is to sort out his name and the dedications. He is remembered at St Erney near St Germans, and also at North Hill, delightfully situated by the upper Lynher River, just east of Bodmin Moor. At the latter church his name is more correctly recorded as Saint Terney (Terninus in the Latin form) – the letter T twice over seems to have been too much for generations of parishioners at St Erney.

ERTH. The parish of St Erth takes in part of what is now Hayle, but the village itself is pleasantly rural. The name comes from Erc, which is Irish, and it is possible that he is the Saint Erc who was converted by Saint Patrick and became Bishop of Slane. He would have been among one group of Irish saints who came to the Hayle estuary and who were commemorated in the neighbourhood; mediaeval tradition speaks of him as the brother of Saint Ia and Saint Uny. Feast day: October 31st.

ERVAN. The original dedication of this church in the country south-west of the Camel estuary is probably that of Erbyn, who was said to have been the father of Saint Selevan, see his entry. However, it acquired a dedication to Saint Hermes – see Erme in Part III.

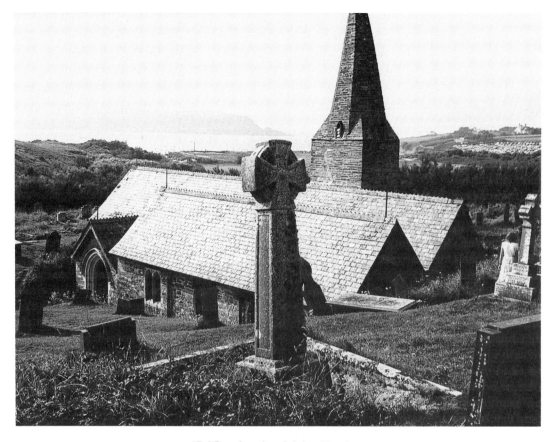

17. The church of Saint Enodoc.

EUNY. See Uny.

EVAL. St Eval is probably best remembered as an aerodrome. RAF St Eval played a notable part in coastal defence and short-distance attack in the War of 1939-45, and the church still serves the nearby air-station, RAF, with a civil air-line section, of St Mawgan. Standing up bravely in the bleak storm-swept landscape near the coast, the tower was once an important sea-mark for shipping. As such, it was rebuilt in the eighteenth century, by subscription of Bristol merchants. It is a pity we know nothing of the man whose religious foundation has been so connected with various kinds of transport and travel.

EWE. See under Feock below.

FEOCK. There is no clear information about the patron of Feock, which looks down on Carrick Roads in the lower River Fal. It is possible that he was the same person as Saint Maeoc, known to have been a hermit in Brittany. In the seventeenth century there was a late mediaeval window still surviving in the church, portraying the saint as a priest with the family, who no doubt gave the window, kneeling in prayer. However, early mediaeval calendars give the name in feminine form – Sancta Feoca.

Women saints are of course honoured as much as men, but there seems to have been an especial enthusiasm for feminine patrons in Cornwall in mediaeval times, as others of whom we know nothing except that we think they were men are apparently treated as women in the calendars. Three examples are Saint Ewe, Saint Wendron and Saint Stediana of Stithians. It is to be remembered that all possible research has not necessarily been done. We may yet gather some information about Saint Morenna of Lamorran, for instance, Saint Ladoca whose well is remembered in the name of a farm at Ladock, and the masculine Saint Pinnock.

FILI is the saint of Philleigh on the left of the River Fal, not far from the King Harry Ferry. On the other side there is Kea and the two seem to have been companions in their work. Just east of Bideford in north Devon are Landkey (the *Lan* of Kea – see Place Names 3, p. 141) and Filleigh; and their names are associated again in Brittany. Fili may have come from Wales where he was honoured.

FIMBARRUS. The traditional patron of Fowey is the Irish abbot-bishop Saint Finbarr, founder of the important diocese of Cork, although there may have been a Barry there who was perhaps one of the sons of Brychan and an uncle of Saint Cadoc (see Adwen, and also Nicholas in Part III). Complications arise because Finbarr, or Fimbarrus at Fowey, is also familiarly referred to as Barry. There is no reason, of course, why Finbarr should not have visited Fowey. He was a great traveller. The Island of Barra in the Outer Hebrides, where he founded Cille Bharra, a revered monastic centre, was named after him. He visited Saint David in south Wales, and it is said that the two made a pilgrimage to Rome together. We may remember that the easiest and most popular route for such travellers to the European continent was across the 'neck' of land from the Padstow estuary to the Fowey estuary. Feast day: September 25th.

GENNYS. There may have been a Celtic patron by the cliffs of St Gennys of north-east Cornwall. On the other hand, there was a Saint Genesius of Arles, who was martyred about AD 250. He was a clerk in the local government, and declared himself a Christian when required officially to write out an edict against Christians sent from the emperor in Rome. Devotion to certain early saints became especially popular in mediaeval times (see for example Cornelly in Part III). However, the honouring of Saint Genesius spread very fast, and Arles was a great centre of Christianity in the later Roman Empire; the first Council of Arles in 314 was attended by bishops from Britain. So it is possible that we have here a dedication which goes back to the Christianity of the Roman Empire. In fact, as a man of what the Romans called *the* Province, Provence in the south of France, Genesius would have been a Celt. Feast day (in Cornwall): May 2nd.

GERENT. An account of the patron of Gerrans, not far from St Mawes, is complicated by the fact that this was a popular name which we meet under varying forms. So it has first to be clarified that, while Gerent was a King in Cornwall, he lived a good deal earlier than the King Geruntius (in Latin form) to whom the learned Saxon bishop, Saint Aldhelm, wrote an important letter on church matters in 704. It appears that Saint Gerent's great hall of residence was in what became the parish of Gerrans. Unlike Constantine, for instance, who became famed for his holiness more especially after he had become a hermit or a monk, it is precisely as a king that Saint Gerent made his impression. He is remembered in Brittany, but especially in Wales where he is found in the very ancient tales which are the beginnings of the stories of King Arthur and his

Knights. In the later developments of these tales we know him as Sir Geraint.

Gerent forms a kind of centre-piece of an important Cornish family, the whole making something of a contrast to so many men and women coming from Ireland and Wales. We can trace with some confidence the line through Lud, Saint Gerent, Saint Erbyn, Saint Just and Saint Selevan, to Saint Cuby – five generations.

GERMANUS. The patron of St Germans and of Rame, both in south-east Cornwall, and also of Germansweek in north Devon, is a figure of international importance, who had especial connections with Britain during the period when the Roman Empire was gradually collapsing. (See also Part I.)

He was a man of Auxerre in Roman Gaul, and therefore, if we are anxious about such matters, was a Celt. He was a lawyer in Rome, and then a high local government official in Auxerre, before being chosen as its bishop. Twice at the Pope's request he went to Britain to take a leading role in combating the heresy named after the Briton Pelagius, which took a dangerously naive view of the degree to which man can deal with the evil in his nature without divine help. During his second visit, he led the Britons in the famous Alleluia Victory against marauding pagan peoples, who were becoming more and more daring in their assaults on Britain. By what might be called the strategic use of the acclamation 'Alleluia!', shouted in such a way as to give the impression of numerous forces, a bloodless victory was won, for the enemy simply turned and fled. While in Britain, he gave thanks at the tomb of Saint Alban, martyred in the third century, probably during the persecution of the emperor Diocletian – a British saint, therefore, of very early times. (His shrine survived the pagan Saxon invasions, and became the centre of the town of St Albans when the early English were Christianized.)

The widespread influence of Germanus can be seen in that he taught Saint Patrick and maybe Saint Illtud – central to the conversion of Ireland and Wales. In Cornwall, he is credited with having personally founded the church and monastery named after him at St Germans. Certainly it was regarded as very important, as it was here that the English king, Athelstan, created the first local bishopric of the non-Celtic type and under English jurisdiction, respecting the existence of the Celtic monastery, and choosing a Cornishman, Conan, to be the first bishop. Feast day: July 31st.

GERMOE. The peaceful hamlet of Germoe is not far from Breage, and the saint is said to be one of the group of missionaries who came over from Ireland with Saint Breaca, landing in the neighbourhood of Hayle. He was known in mediaeval times also as King Germochus (in Latin form) and there is a fine little fifteenth century building in the churchyard known as King Germoe's or Saint Germoe's Chair. This bears witness to some strong local tradition, now unfortunately lost to us. The three-fold seating arrangement suggests usage by priest, deacon and sub-deacon during the popular outdoor rites and celebrations.

GLUVIAS. Not much is known of the patron of St Gluvias by Penryn, but he had distinguished relations, being, it is said, a brother to Cadoc celebrated in Wales, and a nephew of Cornwall's perhaps still more celebrated Saint Petroc, himself of course a Welshman; see their entries. It is a pleasant reminder of the family connections, like the friendships, so often found among the Celtic saints. Feast day: May 3rd.

GONAND. There are no surviving records of the patron of Roche, on the north side of the china clay country; the name may be related to Conan (see that entry).

The little town takes its name from the hermit's rock in the parish, one of the most fascinating religious monuments of Cornwall. On the massive outcrop of granite, partly hewn out of the rock, is the hermit's cell or living quarters, and above this are the remains of the chapel of Saint Michael, built in 1409. This of course is quite late, historically speaking, and it may be supposed that there had long been a hermitage on the rock, perhaps originally that of Saint Gonand himself.

The form of the word Roche is presumably a reflection of the very widespread use of French in mediaeval times, when there were such great political and personal connections across the Channel. There was a very popular Saint Rock or Roch from southern France, who is portrayed in a wall painting in the church of St Thomas by Launceston, but no evidence has, so far at least, been found of any relation either with Roche or with Rock across the Camel estuary from Padstow. The patron of Porthilly by Rock is Saint Michael.

GORAN. According to the Life of Saint Petroc, there was a Saint Wron who was a hermit at what is now Bodmin, who gave Petroc divinely inspired hospitality, and then obligingly 'departed to seek a new abode for himself'. (Thus began the celebrated association of the place with Saint Petroc.) He left his name at Saint Guron's Well in what is now the churchyard at Bodmin, while his new abode, also bearing a form of his name, became Gorran near Mevagissey. What is now called Gorran Haven, however, has no connection with Gorran churchtown. It was originally named Porth East, and East is a popular form of Just to whom its chapel is dedicated. Feast day: May 7th.

GULVAL. See Wolvela.

GUNWALLOE. See Winwaloe.

GWENNAP. See Wennap.

GWINEAR was a leader among the groups of Irish missionaries who came to the lands near the Hayle Estuary. According to the surviving accounts, he was a brother to Piala (commemorated at Phillack, see her entry). He is remembered as a martyr, as he and a number of his companions were put to death by a local king known as Teudrig or Tudor – 'fearing lest they might convert his people to the faith of Christ'. A popular tale narrates that after his beheading Gwinear picked up his head and walked away with it; later, he appeared to a man in a dream, so that he might go and bury the saint's body and those of his fellow martyrs, which had been left in a field by the wood where they were struck down. Teudrig 'the Tyrant of dark Riviere' appears again in the mediaeval life of Meryadoc (see his entry) as the typical martial enemy of Christians at that time, that is to say, a Muslim. Obviously he was not this historically, and in fact it has been suggested that he himself was a Christian, well dug into the life of his land and resenting intrusion. Henry Jenner remarked to G.K. Chesterton that he did not believe these Irish missionaries were martyred by heathens but by 'rather slack Christians'. Feast day: March 23rd.

GWITHIAN. We have no records of Gwithian or Gothian, patron of the hamlet a little inland from Gwithian Towans and overlooked by Godrevy Point, with the lighthouse on Godrevy Island out in the bay. However, the sense of the ancient past is strong there: in the comparatively level sand, through which the

mineral-coloured Red River flows down to the sea, there was once by tradition a 'city' that is, a town of importance. In the sandhills, the towans themselves, an assiduous or lucky searcher may come across remains of Saint Gwithian's chapel or oratory, sometimes buried but sometimes revealed by the shifting sands.

HYDROC. The place-name Lanhydrock suggests that a man of this name founded a religious centre, perhaps a small monastery, where the small church and great house now stand. In mediaeval times the parish was administered by the Priory of St Petroc at Bodmin, which controlled extensive areas of land. A Bodmin Calendar of 1478 includes an entry for St Ydrocus, which indicates a living mediaeval veneration. Feast day: May 5th.

IA. St Ives in west Cornwall is known in Cornish as Porth Ia. This maiden 'of noble birth' came from Ireland, probably with the group led by Gwinear. But she was not one of the martyrs, having settled a little way away on the land of a well-disposed king or chieftain, named Dinan, who indeed built her a church. She was a celebrated saint at least in west Cornwall and her tomb was in the church at St Ives in mediaeval times, presumably an altar-tomb in the classic, traditional style (see Part I, and Endelienta). Perhaps because of the fame of St Ives as a place of beauty and in due course a holiday resort, the tale of Saint Ia floating over the sea to Cornwall on a wondrously enlarged leaf is still well known, compared with legends once told about many other of the saints. Sometimes in popular fancy this gets changed into a millstone; this anecdote is also recounted of Saint Piran in particular, and others too. Legends are often appealing and indeed inspiring, but it is a great pity that

18. The patron of St Ives in the Catholic church; carved out of a piece of driftwood by Faust Lang, a member of an Oberammergau family who settled in St Ives.

to many otherwise well informed, and devout, people, 'Cornish Saints' should do no more than conjure up pictures of men and women floating over from Ireland on round pieces of stone. Feast day: February 3rd.

ILDIERNA. William of Worcester, in his visit to Cornwall in the fifteenth century, was told that the remains of the bishop Saint Hyldren were enshrined in the church at Lansallos. Some records, however, suggest that the saint was a woman – although the apparently feminine ending to the Latin form of a name can be misleading. Further controversy has arisen over the name of this place, situated near the cliffs between Polruan and Polperro. *Lan* at least gives us a religious centre (see Place Names 3, p. 141). Feast day: February 1st.

ILLOGAN. We have no written accounts of the name-saint of Illogan, between Redruth and the north coast of Cornwall. However this is one of the churches in which William of Worcester in the late fifteenth century notes that the tomb of the saint was still preserved and honoured. This preservation of a burial place over many hundreds of years is of course perfectly possible, given uninterrupted community life and deep-rooted beliefs. Even in England, the tomb of Saint Edward the Confessor in Westminster Abbey has survived over nine hundred years of eventful history.

ISSEY appears in the lists of the Children of Brychan (see Adwen) and St Issey, between Wadebridge and Padstow, is in the general area where a number of them are found. He is also half of Mevagissey! (See Meva.)

IVE. See Ivo in Part III.

JULIOT. Her name appears in various forms: Julitta, Gilt, and she may have been the Juliana in the lists of the Children of Brychan (see Adwen). Like so many of them, her name is found in the north Cornwall area: she is honoured at Lanteglos by Camelford as well as at St Juliot near Boscastle. Most interestingly of all, she may be the patron of the chapel on the 'island' at Tintagel; its remains are now well tidied up and cared for. It is possible that she was directly connected with the Celtic monastery there, which should not be overlooked by those seeking King Arthur. The ruins of the magnificently situated castle are, of course, mediaeval, and it is Geoffrey of Monmouth's *History of the Kings of Britain*, in the early twelfth century, which distinctly places Arthur there. At this distance in time, we cannot always be sure how much he is drawing on older stories and how much, though we know it was a good deal, that he made up himself. He was not, of course, writing history in the contemporary sense of the word. Arthur did exist and was a leader in the British Christian struggles with the invading heathen Germanic peoples. From the finds of archaeology we know that during the same period Tintagel monastery was an important Christian centre, in touch with other parts of the Christian world. That there should have been some kind of British fortification there as well seems probable, in the light of both geography and history. On either count, the valiant and dedicated Arthur could have been there. It is a possible association joined with the others which exist between Arthur and Cornwall – tradition in the popular sense, but not therefore treated as valueless by researchers. Feast day: June 16th.

JUST. He gives his name to two notable places, very different from each other: St Just in Penwith on the moorland not far from Land's End, and the lovely St Just in Roseland on a little creek of the lower River Fal. It is probable that he was the Yestin or Justin who was a son of Saint Gerent, and therefore a member of

19. Saint Juliot's church in spring time at Lanteglos by Camelford.

the Cornish family of saints of whom we can trace an outline. We know from William of Worcester that in the fifteenth century the church at St Just in Penwith claimed to enshrine his relics, nor indeed is there any impossibility about this kind of preservation as long as no upheaval, natural or man-made, occurs to disturb them. The church now houses a very ancient tombstone with a Latin inscription and one of the forms of the Chi/Rho cross (see p. 138). In the heart of the town is a *plen-an-gwary* or playing place; that is, one of the permanent open-air theatres of mediaeval Cornwall (which are overlooked when it is stated that permanent constructions first came in with the Elizabethan theatre). We should envisage here vivid dramatic celebrations of their patron saint, as well as of other community feasts, bringing together Christian teachings and the lives of the local people.

KEA. Kea (which has had three churches) and Philleigh are on opposite sides of the River Fal, and it seems that the saints of the two places were friends. Kea, however, is particularly interesting in his own right. We have to bear in mind that the Christian Church was established in Britain during the Roman Empire, and that the invasion by Angles, Saxons and Jutes was a long process, so that a Celtic area existed for some time in Devon and north Somerset (linking up with Wales – see Part I). We do not know precisely when Glastonbury Abbey was founded on what was then a kind of island, with its remarkable Tor, in the marshy lakes of north Somerset. But it is a very ancient foundation indeed, certainly Celtic and possibly Romano-British. It became a Saxon monastery under the great King Ine of Wessex, was one of the famous and most influential monasteries of the Middle Ages, and played an historic role in the religious struggles of the sixteenth century.

It is only to be expected that monks from the original Celtic monastery would have followed the custom of their fellows at the time and gone out to other parts of the Celtic world. Kea it appears was one of them; while it was probably in Somerset that he came to know Saint Gildas, the British monk and pupil of Saint Illtud, who wrote a not very clear but still valuable account of this sometimes chaotic period.

From early times Glastonbury has also been associated with King Arthur, though a supposed identification of his actual burial place there is mediaeval. Kea himself (it need hardly be said) at one time visited Brittany. He returned to Cornwall, we are told, from his Breton monastery at Cléder, to try to make peace between Arthur and Mordred. Thus he took part in those crucial events when Arthur's work fell apart around him. It is probably he who appears in Arthurian legend as Sir Kay or Kei, King Arthur's steward. All such stories have been much elaborated, but often we are moved, and rightly, by their beauty and humanity. Behind these lie historical facts, and short of details as we are, Kea brings us into contact with important areas of life in this early period. Feast day: October 3rd.

KENWYN. Saint Kenwyn, of the picturesque little church looking down through the trees to Truro, may be Saint Keyne with the Cornish *wyn* (or *gwyn*) added to her name, that is to say: white, shining, blessed, holy. However, the dedication is not certain, and Saint Cuby has also been suggested. (See both their entries.)

KERIA. The form of this name is, as often happens, variable; but Keria is still in use in modern times. She is patron of Egloskerry near Launceston as the name implies (*eglos* – church) and one of the reputed daughters of Brychan, so many of whose children's names are to be found in north Cornwall (see Adwen).

KEVERNE. St Keverne, not far from the cliffs in the Meneage district of the Lizard peninsular, is in an area which was rich in religious life. Meneage itself signifies monastic land, with the associated idea of a place of rest or sanctuary. There was a Celtic monastery at St Keverne; and in the Middle Ages that parish, as it had become, was granted special rights of sanctuary for those pursued by officers of the law, which was one of the ways in which the Church humanized harshness in the state. In the light of all this, it is a pity that we know nothing of Saint Keverne himself. A well known legend of the Lizard district has been retold in the rhyme of 'The Good St Keverne and the Gaunt St Just'. A little hard on Saint Just, as the writer himself admits, for he is accused of stealing Saint Keverne's paten, and he only gives up this plate used in the Mass after Saint Keverne pursues him with the great boulders which can be seen lying where they fell on Tremenheverne Downs! (Keverne has mutated to 'heverne'.)

St Keverne Church

From one lone Shrine the tolling of a bell
Is calling souls to pray,
And, ere the dying day
Fades into night, prayer shall all fears dispel.

The sinful tumult of the day must cease,
And man be satisfied
If he at eventide
Submits his soul unto the sway of Peace.

Jebus Bickle

KEW. St Kew in the country north of Wadebridge was originally Lan Docco, that is to say, here, the monastery of Docco (for *Lan* see Place Names 3, p. 141). There is a moving account in the Life of Saint Samson of how Samson came to this place with members of his family and other companions of their first landing in Cornwall, and were met with great humility by a spokesman of the monastic brothers: 'A wise man . . . Juniavus by name – who himself was also named amongst them, in the British language, Light'. (In Cornish this might be *Lughes*, literally 'lightning' – but also used for 'bright or shining one'; *Gwyn*, *Golow*, can also include the sense of a spiritual brightness.) Docco came from Gwent (south Wales) and Kew was his sister; that they worked closely together is suggested by the fact there was a chapel dedicated to Saint Kew close by the church. In the fifteenth century this outside chapel was given up in favour of one part of the enlarged church building itself. For no known reason, Saint Kew, having moved in, took over the name of the whole place; the church itself can be regarded as under the patronage of both sister and brother. Feast day: February 8th.

KEYNE. Saint Keyne appears as one of the daughters of Brychan (see Adwen) and also as an aunt of the Welsh Cadoc; their names are found near to each other in a number of places. Statements in a late mediaeval Life of the saint, combined with the study of place-names, produce a general pattern of her life and work, as a consecrated virgin who left Wales first to live in the woods on the left bank of the River Severn. She can be traced in Herefordshire and at Keynsham near Bristol. She made numerous missionary journeys, and in Cornwall is remembered at St Martin by Looe and St Keyne itself between Looe and Liskeard. Her well at crossroads a little way outside the village is in fine condition after restoration, and is often adorned with flowers. It is perhaps a pity so beautiful a spot should be best remembered for an old tale that whichever of a newly married couple should drink of the well first would have domination for life. However, mild silliness is not confined to the more simple minded. A scholarly theory has suggested that the saint must have been a man, because a woman would hardly have done all that hard work and travelling. Feast day: October 8th.

LADOCA. See under Feock.

LEVAN. See Selevan. He is not the saint of Porthleven; see Elwyn.

LUDGVAN. There are various forms of this name, such as Ludewon and that commonly used today, Lewdegran. It has been suggested that it is in fact a simple place-name, but the title of Saint is given in some records. Moreover, there is concrete evidence of a former veneration in the clearly very ancient little carving of a patronal figure built into the upper part of the newer porch, which speaks more directly to us than many words. The church was partially rebuilt in the later Middle Ages, and the dedication was changed to Saint Paul, celebrating the Feast of his Conversion, January 25th. However, what has happened in practice is that it is Ludgvan Feast, commemorating Saint Lewdegran, which is celebrated at the time. This is not 'wrong', though it may be irritating to very orderly minds.

20. The patron of Ludgvan, over the doorway of the porch.

MABYN is traditionally one of the daughters of Brychan (see Adwen). St Mabyn is near Wadebridge in the north Cornwall area where so many of them seem to have settled. Nicholas Roscarrock (see Endelienta) tells us that when the church there was rebuilt in about 1500 an especial hymn was sung in her honour, a reminder that there was more to mediaeval worship than the formal Latin offices, however rich and radiant. Saint Mabyn appears also in another reminder of older community and church life – the windows of St Neot church. She is to be seen in the window presented by 'Wives of the Parish'. Feast day: November 18th.

MADRON. Madron is the ancient mother parish of Penzance which, like a number of places right on the sea, did not grow significantly until fairly recently. Saint Madern, as he is more commonly called, is hard to identify; more likely than the Welsh Saint Padarn or the Irish Saint Madran is the Welsh Mactronus, who founded the important abbey and bishopric at Tréguier in Brittany.

Surviving in Madron parish is his chapel, which makes up for all these doubts about written records. It is there among the trees and flowers, with upstanding walls (though no roof), stone side benches for those who need to sit during the Holy Mysteries, the altar, and also the little natural font, fed by a living stream, for baptism. It is impossible to say that every stone dates back to the saint himself, but it is absurd to imagine that any later work that was done on this very small and simple building would have altered the position of its foundation and original walls and the actual baptistery. (When a new church was built, it was in what is now Madron village.) Even after the religious changes of the sixteenth century the chapel was regarded as in some sense holy, and its water was recorded as bringing about some cures of the sick. Today, the water is often used for christenings and Christian services are sometimes celebrated in the chapel. Madron Well itself, which provides the water for the baptistery, is a little distance away. It has come to be treated as a wishing well. However, it was not only the source of water for the early community but in more recent times, too: in 1750 water from it was channelled down the long hill to form Penzance's first general water supply. Feast day: May 17th.

MANACCA and **MANACUS**. See under Dunstan in Part III.

MAWES. The patron of the picturesque St Mawes, opposite Falmouth, is better known in Brittany, where he is commemorated at Ile Maudez and Lanmodez. There he is associated with Saint Budoc, as in Cornwall. (He may also have sailed to the Isles of Scilly; possibly there was devotion to him there. See map of Scillonia, p. 135.) Feast day: November 18th.

MAWGAN. Saint Mawgan (or Maugan or Meugan) may have been a Welsh missionary bishop, an associate of the two great men Cadoc and Breoc and, like them, known also in Brittany. St Mawgan in Meneage means St Mawgan in the Monastic-Land (see Keverne). Such a title might also be given to St Mawgan in Pydar, for the church nestling in the lovely Vale of Lanherne is itself a successor of a Celtic monastery. It is divided only by a wall from the former Arundell house where Catholic worship never died out, and in which for two hundred years now, Carmelite nuns have maintained the monastic life in Cornwall (see also Part IV). Feast day: September 24th.

MAWNAN. See under Stephen in Part III.

MERRYN. See Marina in Part III.

MERTERIANA is the patron of the church improbably situated on the cliff top

21. Saint Mabyn is not forgotten by the people of Cornwall. The painter was Vic Harvey.

facing Atlantic storms at Tintagel. The village itself is a little distance away, and somewhat more sheltered. Strictly speaking, this is Trevena; Tintagel is only the headland with its castle and monastery, and for that see Saint Juliot. The low and solid Norman church is distinguished by containing an altar in a side chapel with an inscribed altar-stone which has survived from mediaeval times. The centre of devotion to this saint was at nearby Minster, the mother church of Boscastle, which once cherished her shrine. It is suggested that the monks of this more cosy little place originally founded the Trevena church as an outlying chapel. Feast day: April 9th.

MERYADOC or Meryasek, sometimes spelled with an 'i' rather than a 'y', is the patron of Camborne (with Saint Martin since the fifteenth century; see Part III). The great centre of devotion is in the Pontivy area of Brittany, too little known by those who favour only the Breton coast. In one churchyard, for example, is to be found a granite 'tomb' which may have been that of the saint. Not very far away is a church erected on the site of his famous hermitage, where is kept a bell so old that it may have belonged to the saint after whom it is named. In Brittany, also, the names of Meryadoc and Gwinear are found together, as in Cornwall the two parishes of Camborne and Gwinear are next door to each other. This suggests that Meryadoc was a companion of Gwinear and so came to Cornwall in one of the groups of missionaries who landed in the Hayle estuary.

Bewnans Meryasek, the life of Meryasek, gives a different story. This is the only mediaeval saint's play in the Cornish language to have survived. It is mainly set in Brittany but, in the Cornish version, Saint Meryasek sails to Cornwall and makes his way to the chapel of Mary of Camborne:

> *Rag mur y carsen, defry,*
> *guthyl dhymmo oratry*
> *in herwyth chy Marya. . .*

> For indeed greatly would I like
> to make myself an oratory
> close by Mary's house.

After a well of water has sprung up, his prayers bring about miracles of healing. Then he confronts the local tyrant, Teudrig or Tudor, with whom he argues about the truths of the Christian faith, and whose blandishments and threats he outfaces. Warned in a vision, Meryasek escapes to Brittany, after a close shave where he hides from his pursuers under Carrek Veryasek – Meryasek's Rock. This name does not seem to have survived anywhere, though clearly it was known in 1504 when this play was written – or compiled rather, apparently using a Breton original with Cornish additions. It is gratifying to read that Teudrig is later given a thorough beating by the Duke of Cornwall. The whole gives us a good idea of the entertainment through which people expressed their communal life, with its lively mixture of fundamental belief, traditional memories of fact, symbolic wonders, celebration of their own locality, and plenty of humanity, grave and gay. Feast day: June 7th.

MEUBRED. The patron of Cardinham, whose churchyard contains a particularly impressive Celtic cross, is said by popular tradition to have been a hermit from

22. Saint Meryadoc, accompanied by other saints, at Stival (by Pontivy in Brittany).

Ireland. Mediaeval honour paid to him can be seen in the colourful windows of St Neot church, where he appears with Saint Mabyn in the window of Our Lady of Pity (a 'pieta') and the Risen Christ, given by the Wives of the Parish.

MEVA is the saint whose name with Issey, see his entry, makes up the name Mevagissey (Meva-hag-Issey). This delightful double dedication gives rise to pleasant thoughts about the two working together in what is now one of Cornwall's most endearing and in some ways most degraded fishing villages. Of more than this, however, we are not certain, though very possibly he is the same person as Mewan who is to be found nearby; see below.

MEWAN. St Mewan adjoins St Austell; the two saints were great friends. He is best remembered at Saint-Méen in eastern Brittany where he founded a famous monastery, and where his relics are still enshrined (although this would not seem to have been enough for them – see the entry for Petroc). But he is honoured also elsewhere in Brittany, in Normandy, and in other places in France, not least because of the reputation of water dedicated in his name for healing skin diseases, and in particular the fountain he caused to flow at another of his Breton monasteries, at Gael. The mediaeval Breton life of the saint tells us that he came from Gwent in south Wales, was a relative of Saint Samson and accompanied him to Cornwall and Brittany. Much that is recounted is dramatic rather than historical. But it tells us movingly of the love of Saint Mewan and Saint Austell, of their deaths, and how the body of Mewan was waiting in an aura of fragrance for that of Austell, and so the monastic brethren 'buried the blessed godson by his blessed godfather'. Feast day: June 21st.

MINVER. Her name appears in various forms, such as the Latin Menefreda, and she is to be found in the lists of the Children of Brychan (see Adwen). St Endellion is nearby, and Nicholas Roscarrock (see Endelienta) writing at the end of the sixteenth century, records his memory of her hermitage, chapel and holy well at Tredrizzick in a small saucer of land just below the present handsome little churchtown. This gives us a clear idea of the kind of religious settlement made by many of the saints. He repeats, too, various popular tales still surviving in his time. One day, for instance, the Devil made an assault on Minver when she was occupied in combing her hair, but she threw the comb at him with such vigour and sure aim that he fled forthwith. An admirable example of personal action against the powers of evil. Feast day: November 24th.

MORENNA. See under Feock.

MORWENNA. The name of the accepted Celtic patron of Morwenstow, and probably of Marhamchurch not far away, is one which is still occasionally given to girls today. Names are very much a matter of convention, that is to say of what people are used to hearing, and the custom of naming children after the patron of the locality could happily be extended.

Morwenna is given as one of the Children of Brychan (see Adwen) and of course she, and the impressive partly Norman Church in its austerely beautiful surroundings, are hymned by Parson Hawker – himself a notable figure, see Part IV. Indeed, 'the air is eloquent of God', and once upon a time the windows and walls of the church too, of Him and his children. A reflection of this still remains in the wall painting which may be that of Morwenna with a vessel of holy water – blessing a priest? baptizing? The power of baptism, residing in the 'royal priesthood' of Christians as such, in fact in human beings created 'in the image

23. The shrine of Saint Mewan in what is now the parish church
at Saint-Méen in Brittany.

and likeness of God', must have been exercised by these saints when making their religious foundations in areas remote from Christian centres. (The official patron of Morwenstow is Saint John the Baptist; see Part III.)

MULLION. The original patron of Mullion on the Lizard may have been a Breton Saint Mollien, but he was superseded by Saint Melaine who came, also, to be patron of St Mellion in east Cornwall. In fact he, also, was a Breton by birth, though presumably one of the original Celtic (Romano-Gallic) inhabitants, not one of the British refugees to Armorica at the same time who were turning it into Brittany (see Part I). He was a monk whose reputation for wisdom and godliness was such that on the death of Saint Amand, Bishop of Rennes, clergy and laity with one accord chose him as the successor. He was an influential person in a period of extreme social and political confusion, and sometimes violent chaos. In particular, he was respected and valued by the once-barbarous Clovis, King of the Franks, whose conversion to Christianity marked a decisive beginning in a new western European civilization after the disintegration of the Roman Empire. Saint Melaine was buried at Rennes, where his feast is celebrated, and it need not be surprising that his name and story reached Cornwall and took over from what was probably an almost forgotten predecessor. Feast day: November 6th.

MYLOR. The patron of Mylor at the head of the creek off Carrick Roads, also of Linkinhorne, is probably an early Breton abbot-bishop, Saint Meloir. It is pleasant to recognize Breton contributions to Cornish life, so many of the saints having come from Wales and a number from Ireland. More than this, however, it is not possible to say with clarity. Confusion has been caused by the dedication to a Saint Melor at Amesbury in Wiltshire, a prince and a martyr connected with Cornwall and also supposedly a Breton, about whom there have been numerous tales in which little historical fact can be discovered.

NECTAN. There is no parish of Saint Nectan in Cornwall, but nevertheless he was traditionally a leading figure among the children of Brychan, and in mediaeval times was credited with being the eldest son (see Adwen). His name is found in Devon, and also in Brittany, and in Cornwall it is associated with two striking places. There is the beautifully situated St Nectan's chapel near Lostwithiel, which has been put into good order and is cared for by St Winnow parish. St Nectan's Glen is near Tintagel, with a stream flowing down to the sea. In this, at St Nectan's *kieve* or 'hollow', a waterfall cascades into a deep stone basin, under which the saint is said to be buried.

Further up the coast, in what came to be Devon, was Hartland Abbey where Nectan was especially honoured, and the Life of the saint which was read there on his feast day has survived. This charmingly tells us of how his brothers and sisters, who also settled in Cornwall, would gather together at Nectan's dwelling-place just after Christmas, to talk of the things of God. It also recounts his martyrdom by beheading at the hands of two robbers who had gone off with his two cows, 'very good milkers', and whom he thereupon had sought to convert to the Christian faith. The Life is an attractive example of what was told for interest and edification, though it provides less aid to the strictly literal historian.

A page has also survived of a manuscript giving the Mass to be sung on Saint Nectan's Day, June 17th: 'Guarding thy people, O Nectan, companion of the martyrs, pray to the Lord for us, now, and always . . .' He has not been forgotten in the Hartland area, where the Man from the Sea has recently been celebratediin

24. Saint Nectan's *kieve*

in music and poetry.

NEOT. At the place which we call St Neot, there seems to have been originally a shrine of a Saint Gueryr. It is Asser, the Welsh monk, who in his account of his friend King Alfred the Great tells of the king visiting this shrine, and he adds that Saint Neot now lies there too. It has been suggested that the reference to Neot was added later, though this does not necessarily mean that it was not a fact. However, discussion is joined over the identity of this Neot. He may have been a Celtic saint whose name may also be found in nearby Menheniot – the sanctuary of Neot, though the dedication here is to a Saint Lalluwy, which name itself later became Ladislas.

The alternative is by no means impossible remembering that, though there were conflicts, there was no chasm between Christian English and Christian Celts. This identifies the patron of St Neot with a relative of King Alfred, and it was in a Life of this Neot that the story was told of Alfred burning the cakes. He was said to have been a monk of Glastonbury Abbey who, seeking a life of greater solitude, journeyed west and lived in a hermitage in Cornwall. (Similar actions have been taken in our own day.) According to this account, some time after his death the saint appeared to the guardian of the shrine, whom he bade carry his relics elsewhere; eventually they came to rest in a monastery at what came to be called St Neot's, originally in Huntingdon now in Cambridgeshire. The removal of bones of the saints, in whole or in part, from one place to another, sometimes for safety, sometimes at a call to establish a new centre of devotion, is of course a usual enough practice.

In any case, popular local legends of Saint Neot, such as that of the helpful stags mentioned in Part I, are depicted with enormous colour and verve in the splendid glass of the church. This, with its other saints also, and Biblical scenes, should not be missed by anyone who has a chance of visiting St Neot in Cornwall. Feast day: July 31st.

NEULINA is the patron of Newlyn East, inland from Newquay and Perranporth, with a church standing up in a striking round churchyard of very traditional design. It would seem that there is no connection with the Newlyn by Penzance in west Cornwall. Nicholas Roscarrock (see Endelienta) gives a local tradition that she was a maiden, martyred at this place. There is also a Breton story of a Saint Noluen who, with her waiting-woman, crossed the sea from Britain on a leaf, and was martyred near Pontivy. Such accounts tend to combine a number of favourite stories (see for instance Columb and Ia), from which it is hard to sort out fact. But there is, of course, nothing improbable in itself in the memory of the martyrdom of a Christian young woman. Indeed, considering the work they were doing among people of all sorts, in very troubled times, it perhaps speaks well of the early Cornish that there were not more of them.

NEVET. All we can do about the patron of Lanivet, near Bodmin, is to relate him to the Nevet of Lannevet in Brittany. This is another example of the numerous place-name connections, which illustrate how the sea was a link rather than a barrier between Celtic communities.

NON. Her name is found in Altarnun, that handsome little village with its fine church on the edge of Bodmin Moor; there is a dedication at Pelynt, and she is also commemorated in Brittany. In Welsh tradition, Non or Nonna was the mother of Saint David, and it may be noted that Davidstow is not far from Altarnun. Whether they both actually came to Cornwall is not known, but the whole pattern of the lives and work of the Celtic saints, not least as Non was said to be a grand-daughter of King Brychan (see Adwen), makes this quite possible. Feast day (in Cornwall): June 15th.

PATTERN. The man who gave his name to North and South Petherwin, one on each side of Launceston, may have been a well known Welsh abbot-bishop, Saint Padarn. However, there is the attractive possibility that he was a local chieftain who was the father of Saint Constantine, thus providing another example of a dedicated lay person.

PAUL AURELIAN is famed as the bishop of what came to be called after him St Pol de Léon, in Brittany. He was the son of a local king or chieftain in south Wales, and was educated at the celebrated monastic centre of Saint Illtud at Llantwit Major, where his companions included Saint David, Saint Samson and Saint Gildas (see Kea). He was ordained to the priesthood, and a monastery grew up around the little house and chapel he had built. His missionary work among the people led to an appeal that he should become their bishop, but he responded to a divine call to go across the sea. On the way to Brittany he called in at Mount's Bay to visit his sister, Sitofolla. She is possibly the Saint Sativola of Laneast near Launceston who has, also, given her name to Sidwell, now part of Exeter. Feast day: August 2nd. She was living a life of prayer with a few other women, but in an inconveniently public place. According to the story, her 'dearest brother, beloved of God' miraculously established for them a little area of dry land possibly on the edge of Gwavas Lake at Newlyn. Near Newlyn, of course, is the churchtown to which he left his name, Paul.

In Brittany Paul was given the Island of Batz – well known to travellers on the ferry to Roscoff – for his monastic centre, and holiday visitors may still see an embroidered priestly stole preserved there. In due course, it was insisted that he

25. The saint visits the pope, in the mediaeval glass of St Neot church.

26. The cathedral at St Pol de Léon.

be consecrated bishop of Léon a little way inland from Roscoff; and his bell, so important to the Celtic saints, is there with the saint's shrine.

A Life of Pol de Léon was written in 884 by a Breton monk, drawing on an earlier account, which includes both what is obviously factual and what were by that time already becoming almost standard wonders to express a saint's spiritual glory. We hear of the expulsion of a 'dragon' from Batz, but also of the kind of practicality we should expect from these founders and developers of human .communities. A herd of pigs is established from the domestication of a wild sow with a litter, and domestic hives are formed from a swarm of wild bees. Always, the endeavours spring from a ground of prayer. In the Cornish parish, apparently through a later confusion with Saint Paulinus of York, the Feast day is October 10th.

PETROC. Perhaps the most striking witness to the fame and influence of this great saint is the number of dedications, not only in Cornwall but also in Devon and Somerset – once strongly Celtic areas but which became anglicized (see Part I). It is impossible to list them all here, but Timberscombe in Somerset may be mentioned, Dartmouth in far south Devon, and elsewhere in that county: South Brent, Newton St Petroc, Parracombe, Petrockstow, one of the mediaeval churches which adorn Exeter – and relics were also enshrined in the cathedral. There are dedications in Wales, for instance St Petrox and Llanbedrog in Dyfed (Pembrokeshire). Important, too, are the dedications in Brittany such as that of Lopérec near Châteaulin in the district known as Cornouaille, with a statue of the saint on the west front of the fine church and another inside of him protecting a stag from its hunters. He was also honoured in the diocese of Dol along with the celebrated Saint Samson, and not least at Saint-Méen (Saint Mewan) – for when in 1177 the relics of the saint were stolen from their resting place in Bodmin priory, it was to Saint-Méen they were taken! On appeal from the prior of Bodmin the English King Henry II, who was also overlord of much of France, brought pressure to bear, and the relics were restored.

These bones, mainly of the head, were enclosed in a new ivory casket or reliquary of what was then the latest modern design from Sicily. In the sixteenth century the shrine was destroyed but later the reliquary, empty but for a mediaeval candle, turned up again, and after further vicissitudes is now carefully preserved in Bodmin.

The Bodmin Riding custom, featuring a procession with horse riders and garlands gathered from the countryside, was associated with the celebration of the return of Saint Petroc's relics to the town, and a second, July 7th, feast of Saint Thomas Becket (see his entry in Part III). The present Bodmin Riding and Heritage Festival on the first Saturday in July is an extended revival of this, including the old Riding Air and a due acknowledgment of the saint. There has, so far, been no revival centring on the memory of the bell and staff of the saint, which were brought from Padstow to Bodmin and in later times disappeared. These were signs or symbols in the full sacramental sense, that is, objects of daily use embodying a far greater meaning and significance. The staff, a bishop's crozier or pastoral crook for responsibility and authority, was also an aid to walking, that is to say, to normal travelling. The ringing of a bell, as well as a means of calling people together, has always been a sign of the presence of the supernatural. We must remember, too, ages of a fuller humanity than ours, when

27. Saint Petroc and the stag at Lopérec in Cornouaille.

things and actions had not been obscured by a distorted emphasis on spoken and, above all, written words. Thus, we hear in mediaeval times of Saint Petroc's Bell being taken from Bodmin to Liskeard so that people might place their hands on it as part of a legal ceremony.

We possess a good deal of information about the life of Saint Petroc, although the mediaeval lives which have come down to us have to be recognized as containing many fictional legends. He is said to have been the son of a Welsh king or chieftain, whose grandson was Saint Cadoc, and therefore Petroc himself was uncle to Cadoc. The young princeling resolved that he would not seek earthly glory but, rather, the Kingdom of God. With a number of his friends, he was dedicated to the life of the monk, and they went to Ireland to benefit from the education and piety flourishing in the monastic life there, and where he himself is honoured as a religious teacher of their great saint, Kevin. After some years of study they took a ship for Cornwall and landed in the Camel estuary. Here, Petroc visited two hermits, one of whom was a Saint Wethinoc, who gave up his dwelling to Petroc and his companions (Petroc seems to have had this effect on people; see Goran). On this spot Petroc founded his monastic centre, in due course to be called Petroc-stow – Padstow, rather than Lanwethinoc. He was here for very many years and then, like others, made the pilgrimage of his lifetime – to Rome and on to Jerusalem. It is said of Petroc, however, that he went still further, and spent some time living as a hermit on a tiny island in the Indian Ocean. Practically speaking this is not impossible; the amount and extent of travelling before the days of mechanical transport has of course been vastly underestimated, while the search for God by those who have (paradoxical though it may seem) found Him, may lead saints on across the world. That the Irish Saint Brendan and his companions may, and certainly could, have reached America has recently been demonstrated by experiment – which is not to say that America represents the spiritually poetic idea of the Isles of the Blessed, or the Fairy Isle for those who are children of the Kingdom of Heaven.

After his return, Petroc established himself in a new foundation near Padstow, building a chapel and, ever practical, a mill at Nanceventon – the Valley of the Spring or, as the place was also named after him, Little Petherick. His life of prayer was accompanied by good deeds to man and beast; he healed many sick people and, according to certain stories, helped an unhappy dragon who came to him with a splinter in its eye, saved a stag that took refuge with him from its pursuers, and converted to Christianity the 'rich man' Constantine and his huntsmen. The truth remains; though we may wish to distinguish symbolic fiction from literal fact, and use each in its appropriate way.

In due course the saint went on again, founding his little hermitage in what was then moorland country, and almost against his will attracting companions to join him and start another community. This was the beginning of Bodmin – Bosvenegh, the dwelling of the monks – which, when the major part of the community at Padstow moved there later, taking with them the remains, the relics, of their saint, started on its career as one of the most important places in Cornwall and south-west Britain.

When, as a very old man, Petroc knew that he was near death, he set out to revisit and say farewell to his communities. But having visited Little Petherick, he found his life failing him on the short way round to Padstow, and he went for shelter into the home of a man named Rovel and his family. Here, typically on a journey of charity and Christian fellowship, he died. There exists still a farm named Treravel. He was buried at Padstow and, an old Life tells us, close by his tomb there is a spring of living water, which heals eye troubles and inward complaints, if there be faith . . . Petroc has left his name also to Trebetherick, and probably to the local Hundred of Pydar; his also is the dedication of Trevalga between Tintagel and Boscastle, and Egloshayle. Feast day: June 4th.

PIALA is said to have been the sister of Gwinear and thus one of that group of Irish missionaries who came to the Hayle estuary and included also Ia, Uny and their brother Erc. She is the name saint of Phillack, on the towans side of Hayle Pool and a far older settlement than Hayle itself. The church is mediaeval and nineteenth century; but set above the door of the south porch is a little Chi/Rho cross (see p.138) of such antiquity that we might well associate it with the saint herself.

Piala would have been one of those who suffered in the massacre by King Teudrig, whose stronghold was at Riviere very near Phillack church, and where there is now a youth hostel. She is still well remembered, though in the Middle Ages the formal dedication was changed to that of another woman martyr, Saint Felicity. This is not the Felicity who was a companion of Saint Perpetua at Carthage, about whose martyrdom so much is known and beautifully recounted, but a woman of Rome, traditionally the rich widowed mother of seven sons. All were martyred, and Saint Felicity is buried in the catacomb or cemetery on the Salarian Way; her Feast day is November 23rd.

PINNOCK. See under Feock.

PIRAN or, more correctly, Perran, can be regarded in the simplest sense as the most popular saint in Cornwall. However, what we can glean about his life is very slight as he is, unfortunately, one of the saints about whom the ever-useful Life of the Irish Saint Ciaran was brought into play, this time apparently under the impression that Perran and Ciaran were one and the same person. We have, then, to go to place-names and dedications, traditions and customs; witnesses of a kind neglected by too many scholars of the nineteenth century, who assumed an overwhelming importance for things formally written down by 'educated' people, and then were thrown off balance by the discovery that the written word might be inaccurate or even purposely misleading.

Essentially, Piran was one of the saints who made the customary missionary journey from Wales to Cornwall to Brittany, leaving a living impression on each place. In south Wales, as well as popular traditions, there was a mediaeval Chapel of Saint Piran at Cardiff, and this was so honoured that the English King Henry II went there to hear Mass on Low Sunday (the Sunday after Easter Day) when he was visiting the neighbourhood. In Brittany, Piran is widely celebrated. His name is found in a number of dedications and place-names, for example Saint-Perran south of Saint-Brieuc; also in official church calendars, and prayer books for clerics and lay people – the Breviary for the Diocese of Léon and its Book of Hours, where he is referred to as a bishop. At Trézélidé, near St Pol de Léon, Saint Piran, its patron, is commemorated not only by a statue in the church, but also by a wayside shrine, almost a little oratory, with a very simple, impressive statue of the saint, his hands raised in prayer.

No doubt his best known commemoration in Cornwall is Perranporth, a

28. Saint Piran in his wayside shrine near Trézélidé in north Brittany.

place which still retains some of the holiness of beauty in three seasons of the year. We may suppose that Piran landed here, for he founded the first church or chapel in its sandhills or towans: Perranzabuloe, Perran in the sands. And the history of this has been of continual struggle with the encroaching sands – perhaps reflecting a struggle for the souls of the Cornish people, as a modern poet has suggested. The building founded by Piran, the centre of his small monastery, was abandoned in the eleventh century, and in due course completely lost in the sands – although not in folk memory. In about 1800 the shifting sands revealed it once again, and since then there have been attempts to preserve the prized remains in full view, but this has not been found possible, though the impressive ancient cross is still to be seen. On higher ground, a little to the east, a new parish church had been built but, after many hundreds of years, the sands encroached here too, and in the early nineteenth century much of this church was removed to build the third one, fitting snugly into its present position, well inland. In this neighbourhood, too, we find the self-explanatory Perranwell and Perran Coombe.

The obvious and common route across this part of Cornwall to the Fal estuary from which, in due course, to sail to Brittany, also bears the impression of the saint: there is a Perranwell, again, near to Perranarworthal, on an inlet of Restronguet Creek. Further west, he has given his name to Perran Uthnoe and Perran Downs.

During the Middle Ages, the shrine at Perranzabuloe containing relics of Saint Piran was one of the three great places of pilgrimage in Cornwall (with the Holy Trinity Chapel at St Day and St Michael's Mount). In the late thirteenth century, bones of his head and other remains were still preserved, together with his pastoral – and practical – staff or crozier, and small copper bell. These were carried to different parts of the country for festive veneration, not excluding necessary, and perhaps sometimes unnecessary, fund-raising. Later, what had become a highly unfashionable proceeding among the powerful 'progressives' of the time managed to survive the reigns of King Henry VIII and Edward VI, but, after the revival under Queen Mary, not that of Elizabeth I.

The involvement of Piran in Cornish life has shown a strong power of survival. The saint had become especial patron of the Tinners or more generally the miners, at one time the most important single element in the community. Saint Piran's Feast, March 5th, was observed by them as a holiday well into the nineteenth century. The cost book of Great Work Mine, for example, in the parish of Breage with Germoe, shows in the mid-eighteenth century an 'allowance for Perrantide' for every man and boy – like our Christmas bonus. Those who, at any time, kept up merrymaking not wisely but too well were thus often referred to as Perraners!

Becoming increasingly familiar once again is the Cornish flag known as Saint Piran's Cross. The white cross on the black ground is said to symbolize the Gospel shining over falsehood, good over evil, the tin metal among the ore. Such interpretations are often made long after a thing first came into being, which does not mean to say they are valueless.

PRATT. See Part III.

PROBUS. Interestingly, he appears to have been a British Christian, before the age of the Celtic saints. Few such names have survived. (See also under Faith in Part III.) Probus churchtown has considerable interest. The ancient monastery once here was apparently re-founded, like those at St Buryan and Padstow, by the early English King Athelstan, overlord of Cornwall but not a destroyer. The mediaeval church has a magnificent tower, a product like much fine Cornish church work of the early sixteenth century. The traditionally named Golden Aisle refers to the family of nearby Golden Manor, who figure in Cornish and musical history (see Part IV).

RUAN. Locally called Rumon, the patron of Ruan Lanihorne on the upper reaches of the River Fal, and of Ruan Major and Ruan Minor on the Lizard was possibly a monk at Glastonbury with Saint Kea (see his entry). He was honoured also in Devon, and the actual shrine containing his remains was at the great abbey at Tavistock. Such things remind us both of the fact that the Celtic south-west was for a considerable time not confined to Cornwall, and that within Christendom Celt and English share in a religious life. A mediaeval story of Saint Ruan has survived, but this is in fact an adaptation of that of a Breton Saint Ronan, a different person. Feast day: August 30th.

SAMSON. We have an almost uniquely early Life of the patron of Golant on the west bank of the lower Fowey River, and of South Hill, the mother church of Callington. The author tells us that he gained most of his information from a monk in a monastery founded by Saint Samson (it is not clear which one this is). He was a 'religious and venerable old man' who was a relative of Samson and had received information partly gained from Samson's mother, which no doubt is why the Life has so many details of the earlier years.

Samson came from a noble family of south Wales; his father Amon was of Dyfed and his mother Anna of Gwent. Before his birth his parents were divinely informed that their firstborn son was to be 'holy and a high priest' and that his name was to be Samson. The parents nurtured him nobly, in every sense of the word, and the happy little boy very soon said that he wanted to go to 'the school of Christ', though various members of the family maintained that the priestly life was not befitting one of their good birth. However, led again by the word from God, the parents were joyfully confirmed in their hopes and wishes, and the boy was sent to the great monastic school of Saint Illtud at Llanilltud Fawr – Llantwit Major, not far from Cardiff. Illtud had the reputation of being 'of all the Britons the most learned in the Scriptures', in philosophy, and in the other requirements of a liberal education such as Latin, the study of the use of language called rhetoric, music, arithmetic and geometry. He was a great saint and his monastery nursed many a good and holy man.

In due course Samson, who grew in learning illuminated by holiness as he grew in years, was ordained deacon and priest. Then, led by the divine will, he withdrew for a while to a monastery on an island, where he spent his days in working with his hands and in prayer, his nights in 'mystical interpretation of the Holy Scriptures'. This is probably Caldey, just off Tenby, which after the break originating in the sixteenth century has taken up again its long association with the monastic life. Samson was called from this place to return home to his very sick father. He responded at first rather reluctantly – a warning that it is possible to 'settle down' too much even in a life of austerity and apparently complete self-sacrifice. His father recovering, this was the occasion when Samson's family – father and mother and his five brothers, and also his uncle, aunt and cousins – formally devoted themselves to founding religious centres and

29. A mediaeval bench-end, now part of the pulpit in Golant church,
shows a bishop who is probably Saint Samson.

spreading Christianity. Only his young sister was given over to worldly desires; and indeed, in spite of loving care from the family, she took to a life of sin.

After a time, Samson was unanimously chosen abbot of the monastery. From there, he made a visit to Ireland in the company of some Irishmen who had called in on the way back from their pilgrimage to Rome. In Ireland, as elsewhere, 'by him, God gave sight to the blind, healed many lepers, cast out devils, saved many wandering in error . . .' Even in this early and intentionally factual Life, there are references to fierce dragon-like serpents. It is tempting to wonder whether there were in fact a number of Loch Ness type 'monsters' in existence – one of the latter in some form was encountered by Saint Columba. As so often with these and other saints, Samson's activity was followed by another withdrawal into a life of seclusion with God; and again as so often, from this he was called to public work in the Church. He was consecrated bishop at a monastery which it is said had been founded by the great Saint Germanus (see his entry).

It was after this, at Easter-time, that an angelic vision of great splendour informed him that he was to stay no longer in that country, but go beyond the sea. Thus it was that, with his three cousins and a number of other companions, he came to Cornwall. Here we do not have the same quantity of information as is given of his earlier days, but it is all rewarding to look at as it tells us a good deal generally about the lives of Celtic saints. We know that Samson first came to Lan Docco, but at the humble request of the brothers did not stay at the monastery there (see under Kew, and also Part I). In Ireland, Saint Samson had acquired a wheeled vehicle – in the Celtic tongue a *car*; this he used for his travels, presumably for the tired or the sick as it would not take many at a time. After landing in Cornwall he transferred his books and the holy vessels for his priestly and episcopal office into a cart. Thus it would have been quite a little procession which made its way across the central land to the Fowey in order to take ship for the European continent.

Passing through what is now the Hundred of Trigg, Samson came across people paying honour to an idol with a play, music and dancing. These he converted, partly by his loving words and partly by the sign of a miraculous work of healing, and baptized. The writer of the Life says: 'On this hill I have myself stood, and worshipped; and with my fingers I have traced the sign of the cross which Saint Samson by his own hand carved with an iron tool on a standing stone'. After dealing with a serpent which had been terrorizing his converts, Samson stayed in the district for some time, apparently living in a cave which had been the serpent's home and in which a spring of water gushed forth for the needs of the saint and those to succeed him. His companions under his direction established a monastery there. This suggests South Hill rather than Golant; but he must have stayed at the latter place long enough to leave his name in a religious centre, when, having left his monastery in the care of his father, he was making his way to Brittany.

He took with him his cousin Magloire, who shares with Samson the dedication of the great cathedral of Dol, the place of Samson's principal monastic foundation in Brittany, and where above all he is honoured. It may seem odd, then, that the writer of the Life tells us very little of that time. We hear of further miracles, of the aid he gave to resolve the violent family and public troubles of a local king, and also of the fact that he visited the Channel Islands, where a town remembers him by name on Guernsey. (See also under Budoc, the third bishop of Dol.) His widespread influence can be seen in the fact that he visited Paris and probably took part in a Council there in 557. He has also of course given his name to one of the Isles of Scilly; see the map on p. 135.

The writer of the Life was probably composing it for Breton people who wanted to know more about the earlier life of the famous man from across the sea. He says that from Dol Samson 'sowed the seeds of many wonderful works, and founded many monasteries throughout the province; if each one of them were to be described this would lead us beyond the scope of our writing here'. Samson died in peace and joy at Dol, where he is buried. The writer finally concludes with words which may sound a double appeal in times which have become apathetic about either rejoicing in the saints or learning from them: 'Dearest Brethren, take it to heart that, while you reverence the saints by celebrating their honour at yearly festivals, you reverence them also by following them steadfastly in the paths of divine truth and goodness . . .' Feast day: July 28th.

SANCREED in West Penwith is not dedicated to Saint Creed! This would appear to be the complete name, perhaps more correctly Saint Sancred. We know nothing definite of this saint, though there is a mediaeval story that he accidentally killed his father and, in remorse and penance, went to work as a swineherd, a lonely life which would give much opportunity for communing with nature and nature's Creator. Swineherds seem to be popular characters in fairy tales, but it need not be regarded as just an impossible fable. Actions of a similar kind have been taken by people down the ages, and recognized saints among them. The very ancient baptistery, not far from the present church, is of particular interest. It is in the form of a deep well with steep narrow steps, and is a most vivid sign of the immersion in the waters of baptism as going down into the death of Christ and rising again with his resurrection.

SATIVOLA. See under Paul Aurelian.

SELEVAN. This has gone a step further than Sancreed, above – the name of the place has actually become St Levan, at least in written records; it can sound closer to the original in speech. In fact, Selevan seems to be a Celtic form of Solomon, though this is a name from the Old Testament less commonly adopted by Christians than Adam and David, for example. Selevan appears in a family tree as the father of Saint Cuby and himself the son of Saint Erbyn and grandson of Saint Gerent. Another tree reverses the order of Gerent and Erbyn. Whichever was their father, there were apparently three of them: Selevan, Just (see his entry) and a sister, Silwen; and it was, in the simple fashion of the time and place, a Cornish royal family. St Levan is situated in a nook of the West Penwith cliffs, with a stream making its way down to the sea, and the remains of the ancient chapel and a holy well. The parish is now known for its important connections with the world-wide firm of Cable and Wireless at Porthcurno, and the Minack Theatre carved out of the cliffs, a reminder of the open air theatres of Cornish mediaeval times, and as glorious in its setting as that of ancient Delphi. Until very recent times popular legends of its saint lingered on. Once upon a time, for instance, Selevan was visited by a sister and her two children, and the saint served up for them two chad, or young sea-bream, which he had caught while fishing off the rocks. The hungry children ate with such haste that they were choked by the bones. Or, alternatively, it was a moral lesson, because chad had not at first

30. Selevan's fish, the 'chuck-cheelds', on a bench-end in St Levan church.

been considered nice enough for their meal. Apparently St Levan fishermen used to call the chad 'chuck-cheeld' – choke-child, and there are the two fish carved on a bench-end in the church.

SENAN. It is a pity that there is no certainty at all about the name-saint of Sennen, the parish of Sennen Cove with its white sands, and of Land's End. There is the Irish Saint Senan, abbot of a venerable monastery on Inis Cathaig in the Shannon estuary, whose fame spread to Brittany. But there is no known direct connection with the Cornish Sennen, and the few surviving records from mediaeval times seem to give in the Latin a feminine form of the name.

SENARA. Zennor is better known for its mermaid than for its saint. The sea-lady who enticed away the village youth was certainly a popular character, for there she appears on a bench-end – now part of a chair – in the church. In those times, no doubt, there were also plenty of stories of their lady religious patron, but no information has survived. She is certainly in the full tradition of the Celtic saints, for the holy well, Venton Zennor, lies a short distance away, under Zennor Carn.

SITHNEY. William of Worcester, commenting on what he saw in Cornwall in the fifteenth century, states that the burial place of Saint Sithney was then still preserved in the church named after him, near Helston. We have no certain written records of the saint, though we have the common Breton link in that he seems to be Saint Sezni of Brittany. There is a mediaeval Life, but this is an adaptation of a life of the Irish Saint Ciaran, stories of whom seem to have provided a useful source of material for accounts of other saints when either fact or fiction was in short supply. Feast day: August 4th.

STEDIANA. See under Feock.

SULIAN. There is no certainty about the name-saint of Luxulyan. A similar name in various forms – Sulian, Suliau, Sulinus, is found in Wales and Brittany. There is also Saint Julian at Maker, but for this see Part III. In the fifteenth century, we find that the dedication is to Saint Cyricus and Saint Julitta, popular in mediaeval times (see under Saint Veep). Whether this was influenced by the fact that there was a tendency to mix up the names Juliana and Julitta is merely another question emphasizing the dubious distinction of Luxulyan in presenting some of the most difficult problems of identification. Mabe provides another example. The name of the recently restored St Cyors' Well presumably derives from Cyricus.

TEATH. The name also appears as Tetha or Tedda. She is in the lists of the Children of Brychan, and St Teath is in the area of north Cornwall where so many of them apparently lived and worked. Her sister at Advent, for instance, is only a few miles away – see Adwen. Feast day: May 1st.

TUDY. The saint of the serene, self-contained village of St Tudy, north-east of Wadebridge, may have been a companion of Saint Breoc (see his entry) whose name is found not far away.

Presumably he went on to Brittany with Breoc, for his name is also found on the coast not far from Saint-Brieuc. His feast day is May 11th.

UNY. Traditionally, Uny is the brother of Saint Ia and Saint Erc (see Erth), and therefore one of the Irish missionaries, led by Gwinear, who landed in the Hayle estuary. Place-names and dedications indicate that he was a person of some influence. He is patron of Redruth as well as the beautifully situated Lelant (though he may not have been the original founder of the latter) and is associated also with Crowan, and Sancreed parish. That he was martyred, like others of his group, is indicated in the name of Merther Uny for an ancient and important church which existed in Wendron parish. Feast day: February 1st.

VEEP. Nothing is known of the patron of St Veep above Penpol Creek of the lower Fowey River; there is even a doubt as to whether Veep was a man or a woman. In the fourteenth century the church was rededicated to Saint Cyricus and Saint Julitta, a little boy and his mother possibly martyred during the notorious persecutions of the Roman emperor Diocletian, and around whom popular dramatic stories were woven (see also Sulian). Their feast day is June 16th.

VERYAN. See under Buryan, and also Symphorian in Part III.

WENDRON. See under Feock.

WENNA was counted as one of the daughters of Brychan (see Adwen) and the village of St Wenn is in the general area of north Cornwall where so many of his children are to be found. However, either she or her fame penetrated further, as she is also patron of Morval, just inland from Looe on the south-east Cornish coast. Feast day: October 18th.

WENNAP. This is the form of the name-saint of Gwennap which has come into use, although in fact the initial G probably belongs to the original.

The mediaeval Latin implies a woman, and the older and full name of the place, Lanwenep, refers directly to the saint's religious foundation in the area. It is now of course best known for another religious foundation, John Wesley's Gwennap Pit. See Part IV.

WILLOW. William of Worcester, travelling round Cornwall in the later fifteenth century, tells us of the patron of charming Lanteglos by Fowey. According to the popular accounts, this saint, whose name can also be spelled Wyllow or in yet another form Wylloc, was born in Ireland. He came to Fowey, and was piloted by helpful fish across the river and up Pont Pill; he established his hermitage in the countryside at its head. He was slain by an evilly disposed antagonist named Melyn, possibly his own brother; there was a Chapel of Saint Willow at the place (now a farm) named Lamelin, reputedly the place of the martyrdom. The mediaeval church looks down on the scene, and a common type of legend was employed to account for its position: after his beheading, Willow picked up his head and carried it to the site where the church was to be built. As a reminder that there is no need to confine ourselves to the better known saints, it may be remarked that active devotion to Saint Willow has revived in very recent times. Feast day: July 7th.

WINNOW. The patron of the church of St Winnow, in its beautiful situation on the Fowey River as it widens out below Lostwithiel, lived rather later than the great majority of Celtic saints. His life also has a certain difference about it. Winnow, or more correctly perhaps, Winnoc, probably came from Wales, and journeyed across Cornwall by the route of the Camel and Fowey rivers, presumably staying for a while at the place now named after him. However, after visiting Brittany, he went on through what is now France to Flanders. We have a record of his helping to found a monastery at Wormhoudt near Dunkirk in about the year 700. In this area he settled, and his shrine in the place also named after him, Bergues-Saint-Winnoc, was a great place of pilgrimage in mediaeval times. Feast day: November 6th.

WINWALOE. The saint of Landewednack and Gunwalloe probably did have a G to his name, which is given in French as Guénolé, but this is the form commonly used. He was a friend of Saint Budoc and, like him, played an important role in Breton religious life: he founded the great monastery of Landévennec which is in that part of Brittany named Cornouaille. There is some evidence that he was of a Cornish family which had moved to Brittany, where he was born: thus we have an example of a saint coming back to Cornwall from Brittany rather than the much more usual reverse process. Little Landewednack, furthest south on the Lizard, was presumably a small monastery founded from its Breton namesake; and Gunwalloe, protected from the sea only by the sandy towans, bears witness to the honour paid to the saint in the same general area. He is possibly patron also of the lonely Towednack in West Penwith, and is remembered much further east at Tremaine, near Egloskerry. His fame spread further when, during Viking onslaughts, his body, vestments and bell were removed to Montreuil near Boulogne, where his shrine also became known to the English. Today, Landévennec Abbey is the centre for the Cornish/Breton Companions of Saint Guénolé. Feast day: March 3rd.

WOLVELA. The name of the patron of Gulval, still maintaining its identity in face of encroachments from Penzance, no doubt originally had the initial G. The Latin form which has come into common use adopts, as in other similar names, the mutated form G to W, reflecting a custom of the Cornish language. This mediaeval spelling also provides us with a feminine saint. There is a Bosulval in the parish – the Dwelling or House of Wolvela, which could signify the place of her hermitage or little nunnery. However, it has been suggested that the patron is, rather, a Saint Gudwal, a monk once famous in Brittany who was born on the coast of Britain. Perhaps all that may be remarked as far as choice is concerned is that mediaeval favour tended in the direction of women saints and nineteenth and early twentieth century favour in the direction of men!

ZENNOR. See Senara.

31. Saints of Cornwall in the lap of God, St Neot window.

PART III

Mainly Mediaeval

Beata nobis gaudia
Anni reduxit orbita,
Cum Spiritus Paraclitus
Illapsus est apostolis.

Ignis vibrante lumine
Linguae figuram detulit,
Verbis ut essent proflui
Et caritate fervidi.

Linguis loquuntur omnium
Turbae pavent gentilium;
Musto madere deputant
Quos Spiritus repleverat.

Te nunc Deus piissime
Vultu precamur cernuo,
Illapsa nobis caelitus
Largire dona Spiritus.

Again the circling year has brought to us that blessed day of joy, when the Spirit, the Paraclete, came down upon the Apostles. In fire's quivering flame, He took the form of tongues — that eloquent should be their speech, with charity their hearts afire. Amazed were the crowds to hear them speak in every tongue; they were mocked as drunkards of new wine, those whom the Spirit filled. Bending low we pray, most loving God: may the gifts of the Spirit come down upon us from Heaven.

Saint Hilary of Poitiers

MAINLY MEDIAEVAL

The holy people presented in this section are not of course necessarily themselves mediaeval. Their names appear in church dedications recorded in mediaeval times, sometimes attached to churches or chapels which do not as far as surviving records go seem to have had predecessors, the majority, however, replacing or joining earlier Celtic dedications. Over very many centuries not only history but popular tradition can be forgotten. Other saints of Christendom became well known, while no flourishing Christian community could overlook the greatest figures of the New Testament and the foundation of the Church – especially when churches were being built on the sites of ancient chapels or being enlarged, freshly adorned, or rebuilt. The Norman period, and the fifteenth and early sixteenth centuries, were notable times for such activities; but the churches could hardly ever be said to have been static. Dedications did not of course exclude the Almighty. There is Holy Trinity at St Austell, for instance, and at Boyton probably the Holy Name – 'for at the Name of Jesus every knee shall bow . . .', a devotion especially preached by Dominican friars in the thirteenth century. The 'mainly mediaeval' strikes a note of caution. Often we do not know when a dedication actually first came to be used, though we may assume it was a mediaeval adoption. We must bear in mind, however, the period of four hundred years between the Cornish Age of the Saints and the Norman Conquest, when contacts with Christians in early England and on the European continent were growing in influence.

AGNES. The little town of St Agnes with its fine St Agnes Beacon, a landmark for many miles, was once closely connected with Perranzabuloe (see Piran in Part II). However, the mediaeval dedication of the church there is to Saint Agnes, a famous martyr of early Rome. She was a young girl just entering womanhood who consecrated herself wholly to God, proclaimed her Christianity under persecution, and suffered the Roman execution of being stabbed in the throat. She was buried in one of the Christian catacombs; her tomb was preserved and a church built over it as soon as the Christian community were emancipated from legal restrictions on public activities. The cluster of buildings known as St Agnes outside the Walls are among the most interesting and beautiful even in Rome.

The name Agnes signifies a lamb, the symbol of purity and, above all, of Jesus Christ as sacrifice for the world. By ancient custom wool from lambs blessed on the feast of Saint Agnes, January 21st, is woven into the *pallium* – the 'yoke,' which is the sign of authority and service placed upon the pope and archbishops.

ANDREW. The Galilean fisherman, unlike some of the Twelve Apostles of whom we hear little but the name, makes marked appearances in the New Testament. It was he who, with 'another disciple', first approached Jesus, after John the Baptist had said to them 'Behold, the Lamb of God', and he brought his brother, Simon Peter, to the Lord. Together, they were formally called: 'Come,

32. Four Apostles, from the restored mediaeval paintings in Gunwalloe church.

follow me: I will make you fishers of men', as they worked on the shore of the Lake of Galilee. Again, he forms a kind of connecting link at a time of high importance when, after the triumphal entry into Jerusalem at the beginning of what we call Holy Week, some Gentiles who had come to the city for the Passover told Philip that they wanted to approach Jesus. Philip thereupon told Andrew, and together they went to their Master. He is mentioned with the other apostles, now eleven, at the beginning of the Acts of the Apostles, as they await the Holy Spirit after the Ascension of Christ.

Andrew's veneration is very widespread, strong in eastern Christendom and Rome and extending throughout the world. He is patron of Russia, and of Scotland whose flag bears the cross saltire – the X shaped cross on which, according to tradition, Saint Andrew was martyred. In mediaeval knightly legend, Saint Andrew of Scotland became one of the Seven Champions of Christendom (see George).

In Cornwall, he has mediaeval commemorations at Tywardreath, Calstock, Stratton and nearby Launcells. The three former names give no clue about earlier history (Tywardreath means house on the strand) but Launcells suggests a Celtic religious foundation. Feast day: November 30th.

ANNE. From very early times the mother and father of the Virgin Mary have been given the names of Anne (or Ann) and Joachim although we have no sure evidence of this. In any case, they have been honoured as the parents of the maiden chosen to bear God Incarnate in the world. The dedication, like the devotion, is a popular one; she is patron of all Brittany. In Cornwall, there is the hamlet of St Ann's Chapel just west of Gunnislake, St Ann's near Landulph, and

St Ann's chapel at East Looe (a newer building but deriving its dedication from mediaeval times). At Whitstone the church shares its dedication with Saint Nicholas (see his entry) where there is also a Saint Anne's Well, reminding us that it is not only the Celtic saints who are associated with the waters of physical and spiritual life. Feast day – the Parents of the Blessed Virgin Mary: July 26th. (Byzantine Calendar: July 25th.)

ANTHONY. We need to look at this name from the point of view of three different places. The mediaeval dedication of St Anthony in Meneage may have been suggested by an earlier Cornish name, Lanyntenyn – Meneage was an area of monasteries (see Mawgan in Part II). In due course, the patron became the great Anthony, or Antony, of Egypt who was born in AD 251. This was an increasingly Christianized area of the Roman Empire, and Anthony was one of the many hermits living in the desert, seeking closer union with God, and thus becoming vehicles of grace for the world. His decisive work was to gather some of the 'solitaries' together into partially organized communities over which he had a modified authority, thus providing the groundwork for the growth of monasticism – the communal families with a definite pattern of life whose influence in past and present is immeasurable. The life of a 'desert father' was austere in the extreme but Anthony lived to a robust old age and died at just over the age of a hundred. He was widely known and revered in his own time, and became later one of the most popular saints. Especially enjoyed were the accounts of how he surmounted his Temptations, in dramatic, sometimes lurid, stories, poems and pictures, deriving nevertheless from real experiences. There is a habit today, to our great cost, to think overwhelmingly in terms of physical good works, with 'religion' to give us a little boost on the way; but actual evil is spiritual and has to be fought in the spirit. Whether or not it played some part in the original devilish appearances, Saint Anthony's emblem of a little pig was taken up and made in true mediaeval style into something homely and even friendly. The nursing Order of the Hospital Brothers of St Anthony, who wore a T-shaped or Egyptian cross, were often given free feeding rights for their herds of swine in the woods. Parishioners of St Anthony in Meneage had the nickname of Saint Anthony Pigs, and Piggy Feast is locally kept on the Sunday nearest December 26th. The general Feast day is January 17th.

At St Anthony in Roseland there was a twelfth century dedication (in the Latin form) to Saint Antoninus 'King and Martyr'. We know nothing more of him, though there were Celtic saintly kings, and martyrs, as some of the entries in Part II bear witness. Another dedication, about a hundred years later, indicates that Saint Anthony of Egypt is being adopted and honoured.

For the patron of the place named Antony (which is apparently not a personal name), in south-east Cornwall, see James.

BARTHOLOMEW. This is the dedication of the churches at Lostwithiel and at the hamlet of Warleggan superbly situated above the Fowey Valley, on the edge of Bodmin Moor. A number of mediaeval dedications in the mid-Cornwall area (at St Blazey, Liskeard, Looe, St Austell, for example) bear witness to the importance of the flourishing area in that period, when royal earls and dukes of Cornwall held court at Restormel and other castles, and before deep tin and copper mining, and the railways, brought the far west into prominence.

As one of the Twelve Apostles, Saint Bartholomew has always been celebrated,

33. Saint Anthony and his little pig, in the church at Gerend near Mûr de Bretagne.

but there are only short references to him in the Gospels and the Acts of the Apostles, placing him among the Twelve. Even here there is a slight obscurity, which is clarified if we assume that the Bartholomew of Matthew, Mark and Luke is the same as the Nathanael of John. In all their writings he is associated with Philip, but of Nathanael we hear a little more. When Philip spoke to him of Jesus as the Messiah, Nathanael reacted swiftly: 'Can anything worthwhile come out of Nazareth?' (Perhaps he thought more highly of his own town of Cana, also in Galilee.) In striking contrast is the scene that follows. Jesus, on seeing his approach, gave him memorable words of commendation: 'Here is a true Israelite; no deceit is to be found in him', while Nathanael himself, when faced with Christ's knowledge of his life, made one of the great confessions of faith: 'Thou art the Son of God; thou art the King of Israel'. In a climax, Christ made use of this occasion to speak of the glory to come: 'You believe because I told you that I saw you under the fig tree – you will see greater things than that . . . Heaven open, and the angels of God ascending and descending over the Son of Man.'

There is some evidence that Saint Bartholomew preached the Gospel as far east as India. He is especially honoured in Armenia where he was martyred, being flayed alive before being beheaded, and hence his emblem is a butcher's knife. Feast day: August 24th. (Byzantine Calendar: June 11th.)

BENEDICT. His name appears on the Cornish map in the form of St Bennets at Lanivet, a few miles south-west of Bodmin. With a later house in the Gothic style, there are here remains of a mediaeval 'lazar-house' – a home, with a chapel of course, for those permanently afflicted by various diseases going under the then very general term of leprosy. It was dedicated under the title of Saint Benedict; apparently this was the name of its founder and benefactor, who would look to this saint as his patron.

Benedict was born in the Umbrian region of Italy in AD 480, and began his vocation as the greatest of all monastic founders when, as a young student, he fled from the licentiousness and intellectual disruption of semi-pagan/semi-Christian Rome, to seek the truth of God alone in the mountains. From Subiaco and the still more celebrated Monte Cassino, the religious Order which he founded with his twin sister, Saint Scholastica, went out to become the most important single influence in the history of European civilization, and now of course is world-wide. His Rule, or instructions and suggestions for the way of life of the Benedictine monks and nuns, is basically a pattern of Christian living which can be adapted to many circumstances. Prayer is *Opus Dei*, the work of God. Nevertheless, *laborare est orare* – to work is to pray, and 'at certain times the brethren ought to occupy themselves in the labour of their hands, and at others in holy reading'. 'Let all be done with moderation, remembering the less robust'. 'Let loving consideration be given' to the old and to children; 'above all, care is to be given to the sick'. 'Let all guests that come be received like Christ himself . . .' (See also Part I). The feast day on March 21st has now given place to July 11th because the former date always falls in Lent. (Byzantine Calendar: March 14th.)

BLAISE. The patron of St Blazey – a reminder that it is not only Celtic saints after whom Cornish places may be named – was a fourth century martyr under the Roman Empire. Very little is known of him, but accounts agree in stating that he was bishop of Sebastea in Armenia. As with Saint George (see his entry) veneration of Saint Blaise became widespread and popular first of all among

Christians of the eastern Mediterranean countries, then spreading to the west. His intercession was called upon for all the sick, animal as well as human, and in particular for troubles of the throat. The Blessing of Saint Blaise in which, with prayer, two crossed candles are held against the throat, is still sometimes given, especially on his feast day, February 3rd. (Byzantine Calendar: February 11th.)

BRIDGET. There may have been an earlier, local, dedication giving the name to lonely Morvah in West Penwith. But the certain one is Saint Bridget – not, as might be assumed, the renowned Abbess Bridget or Brigid of early Ireland, but the great Bridget of Sweden, 1303-1373. From a noble family, she married and had eight children, among whom (it may cheer parents to know) one was a saint and one something like a criminal. After her husband's death she founded the Order of the Holy Saviour, more commonly known as Bridgettines. As well as general good works their especial duty was prayer and study, with emphasis on the Bible; and, like certain other Orders, they were often organized in double monasteries of men and women, with a woman at the head. The Bridgettine Syon Abbey at South Brent in Devon is a direct descendant of the famous Syon Abbey founded at Isleworth, Middlesex, by King Henry V. Saint Bridget spent much time in Rome, not only caring for the poor but, like other notable mediaeval women, making her voice heard over Church matters in high circles. Feast day: July 23rd.

CATHERINE. This has been the name of a number of remarkable saints, of whom perhaps the best known are the mediaeval Catherine of Siena and the nineteenth century Catherine Labouré to whose obedience to divine inspiration is due the 'miraculous medal' worn or carried by many people today. However, the popular saint of mediaeval times was Catherine of Alexandria, one of the martyrs under the Roman Empire. This – unlike some of those martyrs of whom we have contemporary eye witness accounts – is really all we know of her, though her remains are said to be in the shrine of St Catherine's Eastern Orthodox monastery on Mount Sinai. She was greatly celebrated in the east as well as west, as this suggests, and among the many tales which grew up around her is that which tells how, before her final beheading, an attempt was made to break her on the wheel, this being miraculously frustrated. This torture of course has also been employed in later ages, but it was Saint Catherine's Wheel which became a common emblem – see for example the eastern face of Lostwithiel church tower, not to speak of the catherine wheels which delight firework-loving children.

Temple church on Bodmin Moor, with its obligation to care for wayfarers, was founded by the Knights Templars who took their name from the Temple in Jerusalem. These monk/knights were especially dedicated to defending the Holy Places of Palestine against Muslim invaders, and the protection of pilgrims. When the very success of the Order, its wealth and power, led to a hardly justified suppression by Church authorities influenced by politicians, it was succeeded at Temple, as elsewhere, by the Knights Hospitallers of Saint John of Jerusalem. As well as skilled care of the sick, this Order now works in world disaster areas; the English Association popularly known as the St John's Ambulance Brigade is distantly related. Either Order could have brought from the east the dedication of Temple church to Saint Catherine. Feast day: November 25th.

CLEMENT. Withiel has this distinguished patron as well as the church and district of St Clement between the Truro and Tresillian Rivers. Saint Clement

34. Saint Catherine's wheel on Lostwithiel church tower.

was the third successor of Saint Peter as Bishop of Rome (the Pope). He died –
possibly martyred – at the end of the first century AD, and thus had been in
contact with Christian leaders at the very beginnings of the Church. He is
especially remembered for the letter or Epistle which he sent to the Christian
church in Corinth, successfully healing the dissensions with wisdom, charity and
authority: 'We have gazed into the depths of Divine knowledge; we are bound
to perform in due order all that the Master bade us accomplish . . .' Due to a later
story which speaks of his martyrdom by being bound to an anchor and thrown
into the sea, Saint Clement became a patron of seafarers; he has given his name
to St Clement's Isle by Mousehole (originally Porth Enys – Island Harbour or
Port). There was once a chapel on this tiny island, and it may well have been the
home of a Celtic hermit in earlier times. Trinity House, whose invaluable
activities are part of Cornish seagoing life, was a mediaeval or perhaps still earlier
foundation, and is properly named the Guild of the Holy Trinity and Saint
Clement. Feast day: November 23rd. (Byzantine Calendar: November 24th.)

CORNELLY. The tiny little church at what has come to be called Cornelly, near
Tregony, is named after Saint Cornelius, Pope and Bishop of Rome, who died
in AD 253. During his time in office he had to struggle with harsh teachers of false
doctrine who, for example, maintained that Christians who lapsed from the faith
during the terrifying times of persecution could never be forgiven and received
back again. He himself is venerated as a martyr, in that an outburst of persecution
was responsible for his death: he may have been beheaded, but more probably
died from the hardship of his life when he was banished from Rome.

In Brittany, in particular, various later tales associated Cornelius with the
patronage of horned beasts, the farmers' cattle. The interesting church at Carnac,
a place better known for its multiple rows of prehistoric standing stones, is
dedicated to Saint Cornelius, of whom there is a fine statue on the outer wall
flanked by paintings of two horned beasts. Feast day: September 16th.

DENNIS. The name of St Dennis, an important centre in the china clay area,
is probably derived in the first place from the Cornish *dynas* – a hill fort or castle;
this name appears all over Cornwall, at Pendennis by Falmouth for instance. St
Dennis appears to stand on such a site; while in the name of the actual hill,
Domeliock, we probably have the Damelioc which, with Tintagel, belonged to
King Gorlois in some of the tales of King Arthur.

Saint Denis of France was celebrated in mediaeval times, being regarded as one
of the Seven Champions of Christendom to whom were attached all kinds of
knightly attributes and adventures (see for example also Andrew and George).
It would be natural enough, then, for him to become patron of the church at a
place which already seemed to bear a form of his name. The original Saint Denis,
or Dionysius in Classical form, was a third century missionary bishop and
martyr, who was beheaded in Paris on the celebrated Montmartre – Martyr's
Hill. This is now of course crowned by the great church of the Sacré Coeur as
well as the mediaeval church of Saint Denis, called the artists' church. Over his
burial place there arose the Abbey of Saint Denis, one of the central points of
French history and culture. Feast day: October 9th.

DOMINICK. The name, more usually with its spelling Dominic, is well known
as that of the Spanish founder of the Dominican Order of Friars Preachers, with
scholars, missionaries, nuns, and a branch for lay people. The impetus for his

work was the Albigensian heresy in southern France, which taught people to despise and reject the body and all material things as worthless and evil. This, Dominic with his friars and nuns combatted wholly by prayer, charity and preaching of truth based on sound learning; they took no part in the military attacks which were later let loose, and condemned by the Pope. Soon the Dominican Blackfriars (a rather misleading term since only their cloak and hood are black; the habit as a whole is white) were to be found in many parts of Europe, above all in the universities which were being founded in this great twelfth-thirteenth century period, and in due course in many parts of the world.

In Cornwall, there was a Dominican house at Truro, its site not far from that of the present Catholic church, and there is today a school founded by Dominican nuns at Launceston.

The place St Dominick itself, just west of the River Tamar, was actually named after a Celtic woman saint – traditionally the Irish Dominica who, with her brother Indract (known also at Glastonbury Abbey in Somerset) sailed up the Tamar and settled at what is still known as Chapel Farm. In the circumstances it was inevitable that the famous mediaeval Saint Dominic should in time come to be commonly regarded as the patron saint. This was recognised in 1963 when he was formally adopted as St Dominick's second patron. Feast days: Saint Dominica, May 9th; Saint Dominick, August 8th.

DUNSTAN is the patron of Lanreath on the uplands between the Looe and Fowey Rivers, along with a presumably Celtic Manacus who is pictured in the mediaeval windows of St Neot church. A Saint Manacca also gets a mention at Manaccan, near Helford, in the Middle Ages, but there is no further information about these two.

Saint Dunstan, Archbishop of Canterbury, died less than seventy years before the Norman Conquest. He was a west country man, born near Glastonbury, and he went to school at the great abbey, an English inheritance from a Celtic foundation (see Part I and Kea in Part II). He joined the community as a monk, and later became the major influence in the rebuilding and growth of the country's monastic, educational and social life, laid waste by the ravages of the Vikings. This remarkable and lovable man was also chief counsellor to the kings of Wessex and the designer of the coronation rite of Edgar as King of all England, which is basically the rite still in use today; he was, moreover, an accomplished harp player and singer, and even a skilled metal worker, in particular a bell-founder. In his old age, he was a favourite teacher of the boys at the cathedral school of Canterbury. One of the very great men of English history, his true fame has been much neglected. Feast day: May 19th.

ERME. This name is a form of Hermes, and the saint is patron of St Erme, of what is now called St Ervan (see Part II) and of the original church at Marazion (rebuilt, and rededicated as All Saints). A Greek, he was martyred in Rome under the Empire, but we do not know at what date. He was buried in one of the Christian cemeteries, but hundreds of years later some of his relics were taken north to establish a centre of devotion, which still exists, at Renaix in Belgium. Here provision is made for the mentally sick, who have come for centuries to seek the saint's intercession for deliverance from what the Gospels themselves regard as in one way or another the effects of the spirit of evil. Cornwall probably learned of him direct from the continent of Europe, as there are no English churches dedicated to him. It is to be remembered that contacts across the sea were at least as easy and frequent as the slow land travel up the country. Hermes is most familiar to us as the name of the Greek god with the winged sandals, the Roman Mercury; but it was a common one in the Greek-influenced culture of the Roman Empire: there is a mention of a Hermes in the beautiful list of greetings sent by Saint Paul in the last chapter of his letter to the Romans. Feast day: August 28th.

FAITH, with Nicholas, is patron of the church at Saltash. She was a martyr under the Roman Empire, in France (Roman Gaul); and in mediaeval times was especially honoured in France and England, with various edifying tales celebrating her steadfastness to faith in Christ. Feast day: October 6th.

Such a name can present problems because 'saint' also means in a more general sense 'holy'. Did the three saints, another Faith, Hope and Charity, said to have been martyred in Rome under the Emperor Hadrian, really exist? Or do they rather signify something like the Santa Sophia, the Holy Wisdom who is Jesus Christ, of the great church (now a museum) in Constantinople? We have something of the same situation with Saint Grace, who is joined with Probus in the village of that name. It is an obvious enough name for a Christian, although the general Calendar of Saints gives only a Blessed Gratia, who died in 1508. But reference to Holy Grace – the gift of the life of God to man, seems also a convincing possibility.

FELICITY. See under Piala in Part II.

GEORGE. The attempts of the west by the Crusades to stem the tide of Muslim advance over eastern Christendom and, in particular, to win back and preserve the Holy Land, extended over many centuries. Not all of the time was taken up in fighting battles. Contacts between East and West, including those with Muslim culture which valued ancient Greek learning, were fruitful. In the Christian world, for instance, they had a profound influence on philosophy, while hermits from Mount Carmel coming west led to the development of the Order commonly known as Carmelites, famous for Saint John of the Cross, Saint Teresa of Avila and Saint Thérèse of Lisieux. The westerners discovered in the East a great devotion to Saint George, who is still very popularly represented in icons, in and outside of the churches, and this was brought back to their homes with a new impetus. England adopted him as patron in knightly guise, and he was named one of the Seven Champions of Christendom, repeating the magnificently symbolic story of the slaying of the Dragon and the saving of the innocent and lovely Princess and her city. The red cross on the white ground, a very ancient Christian banner, was named Saint George's flag. It is, therefore, not surprising to find that a mediaeval chapel of Saint George, of which perhaps a few carved stones survive, was built in Lostwithiel.

Looe Island is often called St George's Island, though the reason for this is not clear. Some of the multitude of his legends are vigorously portrayed in the late mediaeval windows of St Neot church. Factually speaking, George is more related to a knight of mediaeval chivalry than any of the other Seven Champions, such as Andrew and David. The very little that we know of him informs us that he was a Christian soldier who was martyred at Lydda, in Palestine, during the later Roman Empire, possibly in the persecution of Diocletian, and his relics were venerated there. Feast day: April 23rd.

GREGORY. We know that little Treneglos church was built in the twelfth century, and that it was administered from the important Benedictine Priory at Tywardreath. The dedication to Saint Gregory (assumed to be Gregory the Great) is not, then, surprising. Born in Rome about AD 540, and dying there in 604, Saint Gregory was a man of great experience, first as chief civil magistrate of the city and then in the service of the Church as a Benedictine monk, before being elected Pope. It was he who called himself as pope 'The servant of the servants of God', a term used by popes ever since, and his fourteen years of service rank among the very greatest in a calling which has produced very remarkable men. To the English he is an especial father, for he sent Saint Augustine and his missionary monks to the pagan Anglo-Saxons. He strengthened the Church everywhere, in the face of widespread wars and tyrannies, and from his reform of its central finances was able to help the victims of these upheavals: refugees, prisoners, the hungry, the sick. He was concerned, too, with the importance of eastern Christendom at a time when divisions between east and west were increasing. He is accounted one of the four supreme Latin 'doctors' or teachers of the Church; his *Regula Pastoralis* (translated into English by King Alfred the Great) still remains an inspired guide for bishops and, through them, parish priests. It could be said that fundamental to all was his work on the liturgy – the formal public worship of the Church, which has formed a basis for its life ever since. If fully carried out, liturgy is sung, and the name Gregorian Chant is often employed for the radiant and exquisite plainsong or plainchant which Saint Gregory influenced, though he did not of course invent – for its roots stretch back into the ancient life of mankind. Feast day: this has recently been removed from March 12th to September 3rd (the day of his episcopal ordination) as the former always falls in Lent.

HILARY. St Hilary church in west Cornwall is best known for the work done in the twentieth century by the Reverend Bernard Walke in reviving customs of much earlier times, notably community religious plays naturalistically performed by ordinary members of the parish, and many contributions to the adornment of the church by local artists and craftsmen. There was probably a previous local dedication, although Hilary himself was a man of very considerable importance who lived before the great age of the Celtic saints and taught Saint Martin of Tours, whose work did so much to form the basis for the age to come (see his entry; also Part I). Saint Hilary came from a cultured family of Poitiers, in fourth century Roman Gaul; he became a Christian and in due course was chosen by popular vote to be bishop of his city. His great public work was his part in combating the heresy of Arianism, favoured at the time by the emperor, and stifling spiritual life from east to west with its reduction of Christ, the living Word, Son of the Father, to some kind of more perfect human creature and tool of God. Hilary was no narrow intellectual; as a bishop he was a warm-hearted father to his people, and, with others of the period, may remind us of Charles Wesley in his composition of poetic hymns which taught and expressed Christian doctrine. Feast day: January 13th.

HUGH. Whatever may be the derivation of the name Quethiock (Cadoc? See Part II), the church in this small village in the east Cornwall countryside received a mediaeval dedication to Saint Hugh of Lincoln. It is not only Celtic saints who have sometimes been neglected in later times; English people are now often unaware of some of the most loved and revered saints of their own history. Hugh in fact came from Burgundy, that area now in France which has been fruitful in holy men and women. He was a monk of the Carthusian Order, one which somewhat resembles the life of Celtic monasteries in that its members live in their own tiny houses grouped together round a centre. As part of his penance for the murder of Thomas Becket, King Henry II established the first English Carthusian monastery at Witham in Somerset, and Hugh of Avalon was asked to come and take charge of the young foundation. In due course, the King pressed Hugh into leaving his monastic home to become Bishop of Lincoln. Like Thomas Becket, though with a more marked sense of humour, Hugh proved himself 'bold as a lion' in protecting the people at large from ill-treatment by the King or his officials. At the same time, the Bishop stood alone in checking mobs of those same people rioting against Jews who were thought to have (as sometimes occurred in the Middle Ages) a privileged place in Lincoln. He waited on the sick in hospital, was a friend to women in need, and loved to play with babies and children. He loved animals too, and the wild swan which would keep him company, feeding from his hand by day and watching over his bed by night, has become his emblem. With all of this went the regular visiting of his vast diocese; while he was responsible – putting in some work with his own hands – for the rebuilding of Lincoln Cathedral, the superb building we know today. It was while visiting the shrine of the martyred Archbishop of Canterbury that it became apparent that severe sickness was taking hold of Saint Hugh and he died at Lincoln's Inn, then the Bishop of Lincoln's London house, in 1200. Feast day: November 17th.

35. Among the artistic contributions to Saint Hilary church is this incident in the life of its patron, painted by Harold Harvey, a later Cornish member of the Newlyn School.

IVO. The saint of St Ive (pronounced Eve) between Liskeard and Callington, and of St Ives, now in Cambridgeshire, has no connection with the Ia of St Ives, Cornwall, nor with the great Breton Yves. In about AD 1001 some bones and tokens of a bishop's office were discovered at Slepe in what was then, and remained until very recently, the Shire of Huntingdon. St Ivo had disclosed these relics of himself in a vision, telling moreover that he was a Persian bishop who had left his comfortable and respected position to live, like many other saints, in a 'desert' countryside far from compatriots or friends. The bones were enshrined in nearby Ramsey Abbey, a famous religious house, from which veneration of the saint went out to other places. The international Order of Knights Templars who were in charge of the Cornish St Ive (to be followed by Knights Hospitallers; see Catherine) may have chosen the dedication. It seems likely that there was an older foundation by a Celtic saint of a fairly similar name: it has been suggested one of the sons of King Brychan (see Adwen in Part II).

The story of Saint Ivo has been one of those viewed with suspicion by academics, influenced it would seem by distaste for a romantic tale. However, it is perhaps hardly adequate to remark that the vision 'may well' have been invented afterwards, or to note that William of Malmesbury, who gave an eye-witness account of a cure which had taken place at the spring flowing where the bones had been found, 'was not always' an accurate historian. There is no call to be crudely credulous, but one thing that Christian history repeatedly demonstrates is that God likes to take conventional people by surprise. Feast day: April 24th.

JAMES has given his name (in Latin form) to Jacobstow, and he is found also at Kilkhampton, and at Antony in the south. This is Saint James the Greater who, with his brother John and Simon Peter, appears on so many occasions of great moment in the Gospels. The sons of Zebedee the fisherman were called by Christ at the Lake of Galilee at the same time as the other fisherman brothers, Peter and Andrew. James and John and Peter witnessed the raising of Jairus' daughter from death and the Transfiguration of Christ, proclaiming his divine glory and foretelling his deliverance of mankind through his death and resurrection; they were chosen to be with Christ as he entered into that work of salvation in the agony of the olive garden at Gethsemane. The history of the very early Church in the Acts of the Apostles tells us how King Herod Agrippa I, seeking to please his subjects in Judaea, killed James the brother of John with the sword; thus James was the first of the Apostles to die for the Lord. This was as early as AD 44, but the story arose that James had done missionary work outside Palestine, had visited Spain, and that his body was taken to Galicia after his martyrdom.

Thus in due course there grew up the great shrine of Saint James at Compostela, the famous pilgrimage centre of mediaeval times, and now central to the Council of Europe's historic cultural routes initiative. The Cornish Bredereth Sen Jago – Pilgrims of Saint James – is researching the many signs of the old pilgrimage routes. With the Council of Europe, St Michael's Way from Lelant church to St Michael's Mount has been established and way-marked. Saint James of Spain is also counted as one of the Seven Champions of Christendom (see George). Feast day: July 25th. (Byzantine Calendar: October 23rd.)

JOHN THE EVANGELIST. The little church in the hamlet so charmingly and perhaps defensively named St John in Cornwall – Plymouth lies across St John's Lake and the Hamoaze – lays claim to the two greatest Johns in Christian history.

Both of these, too, were once commemorated in many Cornish mediaeval chapels. The earlier dedication was to Saint John the Evangelist; see also James above. On one occasion their Master, surely with affectionate humour, named the two fiery and enthusiastic brothers: Boanerges – Sons of Thunder. But the reproofs they earned for their too hasty expectation of a worldly kingdom exclusive of 'enemies' were far from total condemnation, as is seen in the history of both the brothers. This John above all is reverenced as the disciple whom Jesus loved, who was embraced by Jesus at the Last Supper, and who stood by the cross, receiving into his care the Mother of the Lord. He is with Saint Peter in their amazed visit to the empty tomb after the Resurrection, and appears again in episodes in the Acts of the Apostles. Saint Paul speaks of James, Peter and John as pillars of the church in Jerusalem.

Saint John of course is 'the Evangelist' – the writer, in his later years, of the fourth Gospel, with its vivid historical accounts of what he had known as a disciple combined with meditation on 'The Word made Flesh who dwelt amongst us, and whose glory we saw . . . '. His thought on God and on love is central to his three short letters (Epistles), while the visions of the Apocalypse, the Revelation to John, magnificently express the drama of the Church in every age in relation to the mighty events of the ending of the world. Feast day: December 27th. (Byzantine Calendar: September 26th.)

JOHN THE BAPTIST. The second patron of St John in Cornwall has had numerous churches named after him, and many boys especially on the continent of Europe and in Latin America. He is the forerunner of the Messiah, prophesied by Malachy: 'Behold I send my messenger to prepare the way before me! All at once the Lord will visit his temple: the Lord so longed for, welcome bearer of a divine covenant . . . '. He stands thus in a unique position between the Old Covenant or Testament and the New.

In the early chapters of the Gospels the accounts of John are as important as they are dramatic and realistic in detail – when he is asked by soldiers or the police guard how they should amend their lives, he tells them not to bully people, not falsify evidence, and to be content with their pay! John was the son of Zachary, a priest of the Temple, and Elizabeth who was a kinswoman of the Virgin Mary. His conception and birth are accompanied by divine signs, and closely linked in Saint Luke's Gospel with the coming of Jesus. Having been rigorously prepared for his mission, he appears among the people, preaching and baptizing them in the River Jordan, to prepare the way for the Lord. Jesus associates himself with fallen mankind in this baptism also, when the blessing of God is proclaimed, and after this John encourages his followers to become disciples of Jesus. Eventually, John is arrested and imprisoned by Herod Antipas for the public condemnation of Herod's 'marriage' with the wife of his half-brother. Herod was afraid of John's popularity with the people but, in the famous story, he is trapped by his spiteful wife, Herodias, and her dancing daughter, Salome, into having him beheaded. Feast day: June 24th.

JULIAN. It is possible that the original Julian of Maker in far south-east Cornwall, and of the holy well with its tiny mediaeval building near the Cremyll road, was a Celtic saint. There may have been a connection with Luxulyan; (see Sulian in Part II). But there is no doubt about the mediaeval dedication which shares the patronage of the church with St Mary the mother of Jesus. Saint Julian

36. The church of Maker, dedicated to the Virgin Mary and Saint Julian the Hospitaller.

the Hospitaller was an inspiring patron of hospitals, homes for the poor, innkeepers, travellers, boatmen and especially ferrymen – there is an age-old ferry at Cremyll – and of all open-hearted generosity: Chaucer's Franklin, a man of means and position, kept a true open house, sharing his love of good eating and drinking: 'Seint Julian he was in his contree'.

All this derives from a number of legends of which the basic form is that which tells how the nobleman Julian was warned that he would slay his own father and mother, which fate, in mythological fashion, he brought upon himself by his very efforts to avoid it. His wife joins him in his life of penance: 'Right dear love, God forbid that you should go without me; even as I have had joy with you, so I will share pain and heaviness'. They came to a 'great river' by the side of which they built a hostelry for poor people, and themselves ferried people across the water – a vital community service, like bridge building. The day came when they succoured a man, leprous of appearance and half dead with cold, who thereupon returned to Heaven in glory, assuring Julian and his wife that God had accepted their penance. Soon they, too, received their heavenly reward. It seems probable that, as nearly always, there was fact at the start of these popular tales; but, so far at least, no records have been discovered that can give us even a suggestion about a date for the holy couple. The traditional Feast day is February 12th.

LAWRENCE. The hamlet of St Lawrence, outside Bodmin, gained its name from a 'lazar house' established there in mediaeval times. This hospital and home for, especially, poor people suffering from various diseases (not just what we precisely term leprosy today) had the distinction of surviving the destructions of the sixteenth century. By 1809, however, it was in complete disarray, and it was formally closed, its revenues being transferred to Truro Infirmary. But a living tradition continued, and when in 1820 a county asylum was opened between the site of the old community and Bodmin, it was under the name of Saint Lawrence's Hospital. This has had a wide reputation as a centre for the treatment and care of many types of nervous and mental disorders. (It is also worth noting, as we tend to think that the things with which we are familiar are pretty new, that mediaeval Bodmin had two other hospitals as well.)

Lawrence has been one of the most popular saints of the Christian Church. He was one of the Seven Deacons – leading figures in the Church in Rome – and in 258 he was martyred by being placed on a gridiron over a fire. Stories of the supernatural heroism and even humorous cheerfulness with which he endured this slow death have become traditional. But his particular connection with the poor, sick and weak of every kind arises from the beautiful account of what led up to his original arrest. As a Deacon, he was responsible for them and for the welfare of all such people in the local church with moneys in trust. When a greedy Roman official demanded that he produce the treasures of the church for the use of the state, Lawrence brought before his disgusted gaze the blind, the crippled, the decrepit, the lepers, orphans, widows – all in need of loving care. 'These,' said the Saint, 'are the treasures of the Church.' Feast day: August 10th.

LEONARD is the patron of Landulph in far east Cornwall, above the River Tamar, although the name of the place suggests that there was an earlier Celtic founder of a small monastery there. His name has been joined to Saint Cuby (see Part II) at Duloe, and among the mediaeval chapels that at St Ives, nicely situated on the quay, has survived and is now kept in repair. As can be gathered, Leonard was a popular saint. According to his Life, written in the eleventh century, he was a Frankish noble of the following of King Clovis in the sixth century (see Part I). On his conversion to Christianity, he became a hermit and then a monastic founder at what came to be called Saint-Léonard, near Limoges. Through his prayers, Queen Clotilde was safely delivered in a difficult labour, and among other marks of gratitude the King promised, in that period of strife, to release each of his captives whom the Saint himself had visited and interceded for. Thus Saint Leonard became especial patron of women in childbed and prisoners of war, but claims of cures and other benefits granted through his intercession in Heaven ran into many thousands in northern Europe at least until the eighteenth century. A problem for scholars – except for those who simply dismiss such things as 'superstition' – is the apparent lack of evidence before the outburst of devotion produced by the Life. The careful student always bears in mind that only some written records have come down to us. Moreover, there are other kinds of evidence again; remembering Saints Protus and Hyacinth (see Pratt) perhaps a 'dig' at present day Saint-Léonard might reveal something. Feast day: November 6th.

LUKE. The mediaeval chapel of Saint Luke, a mile from Bolventor, suffered during the religious changes of the sixteenth century. In the church-building movement of the nineteenth century, a parish of St Luke was created at Tideford, near St Germans, and the Norman font was brought there from the old St Luke's chapel. (Bolventor, more conveniently on the main road across Bodmin Moor, was itself given a church of the Holy Trinity at about the same time.)

Saint Luke of course is celebrated as the writer of one of the four Gospels. He was not one of the original Jewish disciples of Christ, but a Greek doctor and a friend of Saint Paul with whom he was in Rome, as we hear in Paul's Letters. In the opening of his Gospel, Luke tells of his pains 'to put the story in writing, as it befell', following the accounts of 'the first eye-witnesses', and this Gospel is marked by its human and varied details. It is he who, with certain material from Saint Matthew, gives us the information about the birth and childhood of Christ, and it has been suggested that he came to know the Mother of Jesus in the later years when she was with Saint John the Beloved. Indeed, there is a tradition that he was also a skilled painter, though certain pictures of the Virgin popularly said to have been his work were painted at a later date. It is, however, interesting that there are certain traditions about the appearance of both Jesus and Mary, and Saints Peter and Paul, which have influenced artistic work from early times, as can now be seen in the museums and catacombs of Rome, for instance. Luke continued his invaluable writing work in the Acts of the Apostles, the great historical work on the life of the new-born Church, in which he himself, as the book indicates, took an active role. Feast day: October 18th.

MARINA. The patron of St Merryn, not far from Constantine Bay in north Cornwall, was said in the Middle Ages to be Marina, a saint from Bithynia in the Greek East presumably taking over from a Celtic founder now no longer known. Her story was popular and sensational. When her father entered a monastery he took his daughter with him, disguised as a boy. After his death she remained among the monks, not only undetected but, at one time, being accused of fathering a child and having to do five years' penance. Her sex was only discovered at her death, and her dedicated life being recognized, she was buried with reverence. The girl who had falsely accused the handsome young 'monk' of fornication became possessed by an evil spirit, and was released therefrom on calling on Marina's prayers in Heaven. There are a number of such tales relating to women in the East of the later Roman Empire, and students have too easily yielded to the temptation to regard them as all offshoots of one, obviously fictional, anecdote. We have, however, evidence that such experiences did take place, even though we cannot be sure of detailed facts. As for impossibility – we should remember Pretty Polly Oliver, famed in song, who, searching for her husband, survived life, battle and wounds in the eighteenth century British army without discovery. Feast day (in Cornwall): July 7th.

MARTIN. Saint Martin of Tours is an example of a saint very popular in mediaeval times about whom, as is not always the case, a great deal is known. Indeed, he is one of the central figures in the development of early Christian Europe (see Part I). He lived in the fourth century, when the Roman Empire had started its decline into chaos. Himself a soldier, he was brought up in the finest traditions of the Roman legions and, on becoming a Christian, he vowed to be Christ's soldier, confronting the powers of evil through prayer and fasting, preaching and caring for the people. He served under Saint Hilary at Poitiers (see his entry), in due course was made Bishop of Tours, and overcame violent enemies and many hardships with what has been described as awe-inspiring spiritual power. Through him, the preaching and teaching of monastic life spread through France and beyond; people came to him for counsel and training from all over what was still the Roman Empire, that is from North Africa and eastern Mediterranean countries as well as Europe.

The famous account of how he was converted perhaps demands a little explanation. Riding along one day in his full officer's array he saw a ragged beggar, and, cutting his cloak in half to give to him, suddenly saw in him also the person of Christ. Why half? For one thing, the whole of the ample scarlet mantle would be a real inconvenience to a man walking along the highways. But also the young Martin had a strong sense of right dealing: a Roman officer's outfit was half paid for by the military authorities and half by the individual – Martin willingly gave away what was his own. It is not well known that this event has given European – and world –′ languages a word which it is hard to imagine how we would do without. In due course, Saint Martin's cloak was preserved in a shrine; and in due course again the shrine itself took on the title 'cloak', that is, in popular Latin, *cappella*. This became extended to places of prayer which are not full-scale churches: *kapel* in German for example, *chapelle* in French, chapel in English (with the same form adopted into Cornish).

In Cornwall, Saint Martin is patron of the fine church at Liskeard, of Lewannick, and St Martin by Looe (with St Keyne, see Part II), while the font from the ruins of St Martin's chapel at Respryn on the River Fowey is now in the nineteenth century church at Herodsfoot. This indicates an enthusiastic veneration in mid-Cornwall, with extensions westwards to St Martin in Meneage and to join Meryadoc at Camborne.

Of the many English examples, perhaps little St Martin's in Exeter cathedral close is the most charming; London's St Martin in the Fields is certainly the best known. The most interesting in our context is St Martin's at Canterbury, in which there is still work of the original church, presumably founded from

37. Saint Martin and the Beggar on a chapel at Lermoos in Austria reminds us of the world-wide fame of this saint.

Roman Gaul and certainly maintained by the Gaulish (and therefore Celtic) Christian wife of the pagan Jutish King, whom Saint Augustine found there when he arrived in 597. Thus, Christian life was shining fitfully in Kent at the time of the Celtic Age of the Saints, commemorated by a very early dedication to the saint who did so much for it all. Feast day: November 11th.

MARY. Veneration of the Virgin Mother of the Son-of-God-made-man has been a natural part of Christian life from early times, as paintings in the Roman catacombs bear witness. In Catholic thought she is the second Eve, as Christ is the new Adam, taking her feminine role in the work of redemption even as the original sin of humanity was the work of both woman and man. Thus also, as Christ rose from death with the transfigured and immortal body of the new order of life, so the body of Mary from which he took his flesh knew nothing of the corrupting and disintegrating effects of sin. With her Son, she is already the whole person, showing forth the glory of humanity which shall be at the end of time.

In the Bible we are given, of course, details of the circumstances in which Jesus came into the world: the Annunciation by the angel Gabriel, the words of Elizabeth when her cousin visited her: 'Blessed art thou among women, and blessed is the fruit of thy womb', and Mary's song of praise, the Magnificat. The survival of the feast of Christmas in a secularized society has kept before people's eyes the divine birth at Bethlehem with the marvels of the worshipping shepherds and wise men, and the flight into Egypt from King Herod. Less often alluded to are the events in the Temple of Jerusalem: the Presentation of the first-born son, the prophecies for both him and his mother, and some twelve years later, the boy remaining 'in my Father's house' to converse with the learned teachers of the law. All the while his mother 'kept all these things in her heart'.

We hear of Mary from time to time during Christ's public life; it was for her that he performed his first and perhaps most delightful miracle, the turning of water into wine for the sake of the happiness of a wedding celebration. She was in Jerusalem for the Passover Festival, which was the occasion of the consummation of her Son's mission; she stood with John the Beloved by the cross, and her Son spoke to them both. The Evangelists do not intrude into any meeting that we feel must have taken place between herself and her resurrected Son; of another very personal one we must remember that all that is said is 'the Lord has appeared to Peter'. But at the beginning of the Acts of the Apostles we hear of the apostles waiting in prayer for the coming of the Holy Spirit, and with them 'the women', those known as Jesus' 'brethren', and Mary the Mother of Jesus. There is a tradition that in later years Mary and Saint John lived at Ephesus, one of the great cities of Asia Minor (Turkey) and, after Saint Paul's mission, a Christian centre. It was here that there was probably the first dedication of a public Christian church to Mary, after the General Council in AD 431, which spoke with authority of her nature as Mother of God.

Dedications to Our Lady, Saint Mary, are innumerable; when not of the church itself then frequently of a Lady Chapel or a shrine. In Cornwall, there was the old chapel at Penzance (see Part IV) and the church at Truro of which one aisle was incorporated into the striking nineteenth century Anglican cathedral. There, too, the mediaeval guild, or fraternity, and church dedication of Our Lady of the Portal have been revived at the Catholic church, which joins this venerable dedication with that to Saint Piran. There are the churches of Bradock near the handsome Boconnoc estate in mid-Cornwall, East Looe, Callington, Botus Fleming, Week St Mary, and others such as Sheviock with Saints Peter and Paul. Notable among the once numerous shrines is that of Our Lady of the Park, or Meadow, just outside Liskeard, established by Richard, Earl of Cornwall; this seems to be becoming once again a centre of devotion, focusing on the surviving holy well. Feast days: celebrations of the Blessed Virgin Mary fall into three general forms: those of the year when she is intimately associated with her divine Son, including Christmas, obviously; other feasts acclaiming her grace-full sinlessness and uncorrupted wholeness – the Immaculate Conception, December 8th and the Assumption, August 15th; and innumerable special titles and devotions, some very localized, others world-wide such as the two mentioned above.

MARY MAGDALENE is the patron of the church at Launceston (historically Dunheved; see Stephen) with its beautiful exterior carving, including a representation of the penitential patron saint under the east window: remarkable Cornish craftsmanship in granite. It is easy to forget that the religious changes of the sixteenth century were not initiated until the 1530s; the church building that we have was built early in that century, and work was still going on when the revolution overtook it. An insight into mediaeval life is given in the records where we hear of those doing penance for sin being encouraged to contribute to the Guild of Minstrels, which provided music for the church along with the choir. Mediaeval ecclesiastics did not regard the arts as an irrelevant hobby for those who like that sort of thing.

38. Mary Magdalene with her emblem, the jar of precious ointment, at Launceston church.

Mary of Magdala, in the Gospels, has come to be venerated as the great penitent who penetrated into the heart of love. She was close to Jesus and his companions; Saint Luke tells us that the Lord delivered her from seven evil spirits, and she was one of the group of women who gave practical support as he was travelling around the countryside with his disciples, preaching. We hear that 'standing by the cross of Jesus were his Mother, and his mother's sister, Mary the wife of Cleophas, and Mary Magdalene'. Two days later, Saint John recounts, 'Early in the morning on the first day of the week, while it was still dark, Mary Magdalene went to the tomb, and found the stone moved away from the door'; there follows the infinitely moving meeting between the weeping Mary and her risen Friend and Master.

In western Christendom, the character of Saint Mary Magdalene has been further enriched by a traditional identification with 'the woman who was a sinner' who washed the feet of Christ with her tears, and with Mary the sister of Martha and Lazarus, who sat spellbound, listening, when Christ visited their home in Bethany. This home he filled with joy when he raised Lazarus from death, and it saw him again a few days before the crucifixion. Feast day: July 22nd.

MICHAEL. There are three named archangels honoured by the Christian Church: Saint Michael, Saint Gabriel and Saint Raphael. In the Old Testament, Michael appears in one of the visions in the Book of Daniel as a 'great prince' in the struggle between the powers of good and evil. In the New Testament, the apostle Saint Jude in his Epistle refers to 'the Archangel Michael contending with the devil', and of course there is the celebrated passage in the Revelation of Saint John which tells of the war in Heaven, with Michael and his angels fighting against the dragon and his evil spirits, the fallen angels. As well as his role expressed in the prayer: 'Blessed Michael the Archangel, defend us in the day of battle . . . by the power of God cast down to Hell Satan and all his wicked spirits', there is a very old tradition that he is the guardian of the soul through the perils of death, as is echoed in the well known American folk song 'Michael row the boat ashore' in which, as is common, the River Jordan stands for death.

He was already popularly venerated by the Jews at the time of the forming of the Christian Church, which honoured him from the start. His major feast day is on September 29th (with him are now celebrated also the Archangels Gabriel and Raphael). However, May 8th celebrates the appearing of Saint Michael on Mount Gargano in southern Italy, in about AD 492. From this, combined with the obvious sort of place for a guard and defender, came the exceedingly widespread custom of associating the archangel with notable hills and heights. St Michael's Mount in Cornwall was a centre for Celtic monks; and it was still before the Norman Conquest, under Saint Edward the Confessor, that the monastery there became a dependency of the Benedictine Abbey of the Breton Mont St Michel. In mediaeval times, St Michael's Mount was one of the three most popular Cornish places of pilgrimage (with Saint Piran's shrine at Perran-zabuloe and the Holy Trinity Chapel at St Day). There are churches dedicated to him at Landrake, Lawhitton, Lesnewth, Michaelstow, St Michael Penkivel and St Michael Caerhays. Chapels, it may be said, were all over the place – there was one on Looe Island for instance, and on Roughtor, and see Roche Rock under Gonand in Part II. The badge of Saint Michael, depicting him vanquishing the dragon of evil, was borne by both secular lords and ecclesiastics, notably by

Robert, Count of Mortain, to whom was entrusted the government of Cornwall by his half-brother William the Conqueror. 'I have borne the banner of Saint Michael in battle,' he declared. It is for such reasons that the archangel was, and is, regarded as Patron Saint of Cornwall, though not necessarily the only one (see Part I). He is also called more widely a patron of the Celts.

Saint Michael is patron of Helston, and it is on his feast day of May 8th that the Flora or Furry Dance takes place. The revived popular ceremony of the Hal-an-Tow now includes 'St Michael with his wings outspread . . . who fought the fiend, O'. Welcoming the spring, celebrating the harvest, such things as these are of course deeply human activities and they were not initiated by Christianity. At the same time, there is no reason to condemn – or to praise – them as 'pagan' unless they include the actual worship of pagan deities. Christianity is the fulfilment of humanity, not its denial; hence such celebrations as Helston Furry were a normal part of life in Christendom.

39. The hermitage on Roche Rock with chapel raised up on the rock was dedicated to Saint Michael.

NICHOLAS. Saint Nicholas is of course Santa Claus (Sinte Klaas) that is to say, Father Christmas. He is one of those famous saints about whom little is now known but around whom have grown up a host of good stories, partly because they were already so popular, but also making them still more so. He was Bishop of Myra, an important Romanized town in Asia Minor, in the fourth century.

His relics were enshrined there but taken to southern Italy in 1087, and due to that veneration he is often called Saint Nicholas of Bari. It was at Bari, apparently, that the story originated of his miraculous aid to sailors in danger, and so we find dedications in many seaports. In Cornwall, there is the church at West Looe, the chapel on the 'Island' at St Ives, and the church at Saltash with Saint Faith; his name is also found at Whitstone in far north Cornwall, though the church is formally St Anne's. At the important seaport of Fowey, the church of St Fimbarrus was later dedicated to Saint Nicholas, a usual enough proceeding. Sometimes the later dedication entirely takes over from the earlier, sometimes the two are popularly remembered together; sometimes, as at Fowey, the second does not gain much practical acceptance.

Such tales as his bringing back to life three murdered children whose bodies were hidden in a tub of brine, and of his dropping through the window of their home bags of gold as dowries to enable three young girls to be married, seem to have combined to produce the Saint Nicholas who is patron of children and giver of gifts. In some countries of north Europe he still appears as Bishop Nicholas on his feast day, December 6th, to gently punish naughty children and give presents to the good ones. Dutch immigrants took this tradition to the United States of America. There, gradually, under the influence of a more general demand from people of various backgrounds for something innocently magical, Santa Claus became first the wondrous giver of Christmas presents, and then in due course (the actual meaning of the name being forgotten) Father Christmas, driving his reindeer sleigh through the night skies to land by the chimneys of the sleeping houses, bringing delight to millions of children. It may seem a far cry from a Christian bishop in what we now call Turkey, who lived sixteen hundred years ago, and we may regret the sheer ugliness of much commercial vulgarisation of Father Christmas. But it is one of the most striking examples of the seed which grows into a tree, sometimes of a most unexpected kind, and none the worse for appealing to the imagination, of which the history of Christian people is full.

OLAF. It may seem surprising that the patron of Poughill in north Cornwall should be King Olaf or Olave II of Norway, who was born in AD 995 and was killed in a battle with some rebellious pagan subjects in 1030. But this very vigorous, not to say tough, ruler not only came to be regarded as patron and national hero of his country, with a shrine at which miracles took place, but also became popular elsewhere. We find, for instance, churches dedicated to him in London, York and Exeter. He is also remembered on the Isle of Man, in his time under Norwegian rule. There, King Olaf helped and encouraged the Christian Church, already established through its connections with Ireland and Scotland, notably the great Christian centre of Saint Ninian's at Whithorn from which Man can be plainly seen. Olaf is hardly a conventional idea of a saint – but sanctity is not confined to men and women whose personalities happen to be sweet and gentle, or attractive to people most at home in a library. The saint is a person who has given himself, in the best way that he knows how, to God; and this young Olaf did, in a somewhat violent life among violent enemies, holding the banner of Christianity above the fray, the rallying point for ordinary Christian men and women who had no other community leadership. Feast day: July 29th.

PETER AND PAUL. These greatest of foundation saints of the Christian Church seem at first surprisingly little honoured in Cornish mediaeval dedications, but there were a number of chapels which have since disappeared. At Sheviock, above the Lynher River in south-east Cornwall, they have been joined to Saint Mary the Virgin, and there was a not very successful attempt to re-dedicate Ludgvan to Saint Paul (see Part II).

Any 'summing up' of both these men and their work must be inadequate; only a reading of the New Testament and some knowledge of Christian history and life can do them justice.

Saint Peter was a fisherman of the Lake of Galilee, and brother to Andrew. His original name was Simon, but Our Lord gave him the Aramaic name of Kephas, in Greek πετρος (*petros*) that is, Rock. He and James and John are repeatedly chosen to be witnesses of events of great moment – the raising of the daughter of Jairus from death, the Transfiguration of Christ, the Agony in the Garden of Gethsemane. To him personally are spoken the words 'You are Peter, and upon this rock I will build my Church . . .' That the rock is also our brother man is emphasized by the account of Peter's individual denial of Christ before the Crucifixion. But, again, Peter is chosen by the resurrected Lord: 'Feed my lambs . . . feed my sheep'.

His leading position is evident in the Acts of the Apostles, and indeed it was to him that divine revelation made it plain that the Gospel is not just a developed form of the Jewish religious life but it is to be given to the Gentile peoples. His two Epistles or letters written to the various Christian church communities in what we now call Asia Minor have an especial appeal in their combination of directness, profundity and humanity. How encouraging to hear him remarking of Paul's Epistles that 'there are passages in them which are hard to follow . . .'

Peter eventually made his way to Rome, where he was martyred in the persecutions which were let loose by the Emperor Nero in order to divert the attentions of the populace – enraged by the great fire – from himself. The commonly accepted date is AD 64, and the tradition is that Peter was crucified upside down, an extended mockery of the humilities and agonies of the crucifixion of his Lord which Peter gladly accepted. The place of his burial, now under St Peter's great church or basilica, has recently been excavated, but the tomb was badly damaged by the Saracen sack of Rome in 846, and we cannot be sure that the bones found close by are those of the saint.

Feast day: the solemn feast, i.e. the greatest and most joyful, is of Saints Peter and Paul, June 29th. St Peter's Chair, celebrating him as the first Bishop of Rome (the Pope), is on January 18th. The Church in Rome of St Peter ad Vincula, containing the supposed chains in which the saint was bound when a prisoner, has a celebration on August 1st; this is the central church and house of the venerable order of Canons Regular of the Lateran, at one time successors in Bodmin and other parts of Cornwall of canons of mediaeval times.

One of the most interesting things about **Saint Paul** is that he is an outstanding example of God's work by direct revelation, not simply through 'normal' human means. As the Acts of the Apostles and his own Letters tell us, he was a strict and enthusiastic Pharisee, though also a Roman citizen. Saul, as he then was, was seeking God in His full reality and, like many such, at first met the challenge of Christianity with bitter hostility. A consenting witness to the stoning of Saint Stephen, the first martyr, it was on the road north to Damascus, as he sought to hunt down Christians wherever they were to be found, that Jesus spoke to him out of the sudden glory: 'Saul, Saul why do you persecute me?' – 'Who art thou, Lord?' – 'I am Jesus, whom you are persecuting . . .' Saul replied with the words that were to dominate all the rest of his life: 'Lord, what wilt thou have me do?' One of the most human touches in all of the wonderfully vivid narrative of the Acts is the way that the terrorized Christians at Jerusalem refused to believe in the converted persecutor, and he had to be personally introduced to them by Barnabas.

In due course, Paul was led into his work as Apostle of the Gentiles by an inspired call from the church at Antioch, the great Roman city with a strong Christian community. It is not always easy for people in modern western countries to fully envisage the effect of that work, in which Paul was first accompanied by Barnabas and then others, notably of course Luke, the author of the Book of Acts. If Rome was the centre of the Empire, then only a close second in importance came the countries of the eastern Mediterranean area. Not only Tarsus, but place after place could be described in Paul's own understated Roman manner as 'no mean city'. But of course to Rome itself he did finally go: the Apostle in Chains who made use of the Roman citizen's right of appeal to Caesar from the court of Festus, governor of Judaea. He was freed after some two years' easy custody, in which Romans could come to him, even if he could not go to them. It appears that he went back to visit some of the churches of his foundation and probably west to Spain. He was back in Rome during the persecution of Nero, and was martyred by beheading, traditionally on the same day as Saint Peter. He is buried where the magnificent church or basilica of St Paul outside the Walls now stands.

Quite apart from his own preaching and contacts in person, the influence of Paul's Epistles in his own time and down the ages has been incalculable. Their variety and personal tone is often overlooked. They are not simple academic sources for theology: they include many personal messages, much practical advice and even, for example, the little letter to Philemon asking him to take back a runaway slave without the brutal punishment customary at the time. Feast days: in the Catholic Church with Saint Peter, June 29th. The Conversion of St Paul is January 25th; in our times it completes the Week of Prayer for Christian Unity which opens on January 18th, St Peter's Chair (see above).

PRATT. The church at Blisland, one of the most attractive villages of western Bodmin Moor, has long been known as St Pratt's. It is thought that this must be a popular form of Protus, the church having been dedicated to Saints Protus and Hyacinth since at least the late Middle Ages. Little was known of these two Roman martyrs apart from a reference in a document of the mid-fourth century and a tradition that they were brothers. There are stories of their adventures as slaves to the Lady Eugenia after her conversion to Christianity and the flight of all three from the house of her father, a Roman governor in Egypt. These generally are not regarded as historical, though there are incidents in them of a kind which certainly did take place in fact. However, a striking (though far from unique) example of the archaeological confirmation of ancient writings and traditions occurred when, in 1845, their burial places were found just where they were said to have been, in one of the old Christian cemeteries of Rome. Moreover, while bones and even traces of material were found in that of Saint Hyacinth, who had evidently met his death by burning, the tomb of Protus was empty. This helps to bear out the statement that the relics of Saint Protus had been removed into the city of Rome for veneration in the ninth century, and we hear that parts of them were taken to various places after that time.

Blisland has the only church in Great Britain dedicated to these saints. It has been suggested that Pratt is a form of the name of an earlier and forgotten Celtic saint, but this is less likely as it seems that Saint Adwen (see Part II) was formerly honoured there. Feast day: September 11th.

STEPHEN. As well as being patron of Mawnan with Saint Mawnan himself, who was no doubt a Celt, this famous Biblical saint is honoured also at St Stephen in Brannel in the china clay area, and St Stephen by Saltash, opposite Trematon Castle, once a home of the Earls and Dukes of Cornwall. Most interesting is St Stephen by Launceston. The name Launceston itself is a form of the Cornish Lanstefan, and it originally belonged to the place called St Stephen. This is an almost unique example of a place-name in Cornish – the holy place or 'church' of Stephen – derived from the name of the saint who was not Celtic. It suggests an early and popular dedication to Saint Stephen. At what we now call Launceston, across the deep valley on the opposite hill, there was a fortified settlement from early times, and the importance of the whole area was recognised by the invading West Saxons. After the Conquest, the Count of Mortain was given the position of a kind of overlord of Cornwall by his half-brother, William, Duke of Normandy and King of England. He built a castle at what was then named Dunheved, around which a town was encouraged to grow up, taking over civic and church affairs from the earlier one, and in due course its very name. (The new church there was dedicated to Saint Mary Magdalene; see her entry.) Thus, in that delectable area, we have today a 'St Stephen' on each hill, the old Cornish foundation in English, and the newer mainly English one, in Cornish.

Stephen was the first martyr of the Christian Church, and is also regarded as patron of the order of Deacons, whose nature is a good deal more positive than just providing a stepping-stone to the priesthood. The Acts of the Apostles tell us that he was one of the seven deacons chosen by the Apostles in the first place to care for the needs of the 'Greeks' among the widows in Jerusalem. Many Jews were Greek-speaking, and much influenced by the Hellenized culture of the eastern Mediterranean countries, and the more strictly Jewish Christians were not above making difficulties. Stephen himself was one of the former – 'Stephanos' itself is Greek for 'crown'. 'Full of faith and the Holy Ghost', he soon became a leading figure, bringing converts to the Church through his disputations in particular with members of Greek-speaking synagogues, and the wondrous signs he performed among the people. Pretty soon he was brought to answer for his activities before the Jewish court of the Sanhedrin and the High Priest. His reply forms one of the great statements of the Biblical foundation of the Christian Church, tracing the significance of the patriarchs and prophets through to the advent of 'the Just One, of whom you have been now the betrayers and murderers' – 'and indeed which of the prophets have not your fathers persecuted?' The climax to this, 'Behold I see the Heavens opened and the Son of Man standing on the right hand of God', swiftly brought the penalty for blasphemy, regardless of the Roman governors who reserved the death penalty to themselves – death by stoning. Saul, later to be Saint Paul, stood by approvingly, and looked after the cloaks of those who needed free movement of arms and hands. Saint

Stephen's last words are in essence those of Christian martyrs down the centuries: 'Lord receive my spirit . . . Lord, charge them not with this sin'. Feast day: December 26th. (Byzantine Calendar: December 27th.)

SYMPHORIAN. Two churches have laid claim to this dedication, and both have been contested on historical grounds. The name Veryan – in south Cornwall – is said by some to derive from a shortened form of this saint's name (though see Buryan in Part II). Certainly from the thirteenth century he has been honoured there, his name even being connected with a small bell or *campanicula*, which must surely have once belonged to an early Celtic saint. The relationship with Forrabury near Boscastle may only date from an observation of John Leland (see p. 143) in the early sixteenth century. Records of an earlier dedication do not survive; possibly it was to Saint Merteriana (see Part II). But church communities are not bound to what may, or may not, have happened in generations long past.

The Veryan dedication is the only one certainly known in Great Britain, but Symphorian was famous all over France and in what we now call Belgium, Switzerland, and west Germany. An ancient and beautiful Mass says that 'We honour the most blessed martyr Symphorian, giving God thanks for his triumph and glory . . .' The young man's 'combat in the power of the spirit' took place in Autun, in Roman Gaul, in the second or possibly third century AD, when he refused to revere a statue of the licentious Cybele being borne in procession through the great city. A mob carried him off to the governor who, as often happened, was at first reluctant to take measures against a citizen of good family. But the further argument of the harsh Roman flogging having had no effect on Symphorian's public acclamation of Christianity, the Emperors' edicts were observed and he was sentenced to death. As he was being taken out to the place of execution through a gate, the remains of which still stand, he passed his mother who was standing on the city wall. She cried out to him: 'My son Symphorian! Remember the living God, and fear not! Today life is not taken from you, for it leads to Life Itself . . .' This scene is magnificently depicted in a painting by Ingres in Autun's great cathedral. After his beheading the martyr's body was safely buried, and later a church was built over his tomb. Feast day: August 22nd.

THOMAS THE APOSTLE is patron of St Thomas by Launceston, in the valley between Launceston and St Stephen, the area which came to be called Newport on the little River Kensey which flows into the Tamar. It is a survivor of Launceston's eventful history as it was one of the many chapels administered by the mother church of St Stephen's (see Stephen). This church itself was at first conducted by a priory of canons, as so often in the Middle Ages (see Part I). But in due course this important priory moved down the hill to a site just by St Thomas, with which relations were not always amicable.

The name Thomas means 'twin', and this is repeated in the Gospels in the Greek form – Didymus, though there is no reference to his brother, or sister. He appears in St John's Gospel, most notably in the incidents which have earned him the nickname of Doubting Thomas and at the same time the gratitude of many humble Christians. On the evening of the day of his resurrection, Christ came to the disciples gathered together secretly in fear of the Jerusalem authorities. But Thomas was not there, and when he was told about it he demanded the most basic proof of the Lord's resurrection from death by crucifixion: 'Unless I see the marks of the nails in his hands and put my finger into them, and I put my hand into [the wound in] his side, I will not believe it'. A week later Christ came again, and this time Thomas was there: 'Put forward your finger, see, here are my hands; bring forward your hand and put it into my side. Doubt no longer: Believe.' To Thomas' acclamation 'My Lord and my God!' Christ responded with the words for all the centuries to come: 'Thomas, you believe because you have seen. Blessed are those who have not seen and yet believe'.

As with other Apostles, there are various traditions, some much better supported than others, concerning the missionary activities of Saint Thomas during the early years of the Church. It seems that he went east (it is easy for us to overlook the fact that there was once a flourishing Christian church in Persia). Most remarkable are his connections with India, not of course wholly unknown territory to peoples of the eastern Mediterranean lands. Apart from what seem to be legends, there is the existence on the Malabar Coast in south-western India of a population of Catholic Christian Indians. While it is hardly possible to confirm their claim to have been founded by Saint Thomas himself, there have undoubtedly been Christians there from very early times, with rites and language of worship derived from those in early Persia and Mesopotamia. Feast day: until recently December 21st, now July 3rd. (Byzantine Calendar: October 6th.)

THOMAS BECKET. The murder in 1170 of Thomas Becket, the Archbishop, in Canterbury Cathedral, by supporters of the powerful and irascible King Henry II, evoked one of the most popular movements in Christian history. Not a demand for revenge, but a recognition of the saintliness of Thomas from 'the people of England who acclaimed Thomas as a father in his life and martyr at his death; the people of France and the German cities, of Bohemia, Castille and the States of Italy, who spread that acclamation far and wide; the people of the heights of Armenia who inscribed his name on their role of saints; the people of Iceland, in the northern seas, who sang of God's hero in their sagas'. It is not surprising, then, to find devotion in Cornwall to this vigorous, soldierly man, who had yet the humility and patience to accept death for the Church and people of Christ, rather than fighting back the assault as all the instincts of his temperament must have cried out to do. The distinguished Glasney College, Penryn (see Part I) was under the patronage of Saint Thomas of Canterbury. In the churchyard at Bodmin can be seen the remains of the chapel of the Guild of St Thomas, which also maintained a school as was so often the practice. (Some school 'foundations' of the mid-sixteenth century were in fact re-foundations, made when it was realised just how much had been destroyed; the vast illiteracy of the Middle Ages is a defensive myth of later times.) Inspiringly situated in the grounds of the great house Cotehele, looking down through the trees to glimpses of the River Tamar below, there is a well-preserved and cared for chapel of Saint Thomas Becket. His birthday was on the old feast of Saint Thomas the Apostle, and the date of his martyrdom, and of his principal feast day, is close to it, occurring in the height of the Christmas season: December 29th (see also under Petroc in Part II).

WERBURGA has given her name to Warbstow, which was never an independent parish and is now joined to Jacobstow and Treneglos, all in far north Cornwall. This is an area of strong Saxon influence, as place-names suggest; but even so it is interesting to find a place which has taken its actual name from a saint of the early English Midlands. As so often happens, it probably began with a chapel or shrine dedication initiated by an important individual or some group with an especial devotion to the saint. Certainly Saint Werburga would be an acquisition to any land. She was one of the early English noble or royal ladies who became abbesses of religious houses of women, and sometimes of men too, among whom the most famous is Saint Hilda of Whitby. Their work, from teaching children to educating poets to counselling rulers to encouraging crafts and agriculture to training – and being – missionaries, has been too much overlooked in the present age, on edge about 'equality' but uninterested in the facts of women's nature and achievements. Werburga herself was a daughter of King Wulfhere and his Queen, Saint Ermenilda of Mercia, and she entered a convent at Ely whose abbess was her great-aunt Saint Etheldreda. In due course she had a number of religious houses under her care, and when she died in about AD 700 she was buried by her own wish in that at Hanbury in Staffordshire. The somewhat fitting theme of movement, in the light of the appearance of a dedication in Cornwall, is continued in the fact that her body was later removed to Chester, to save desecration from the marauding Danes. There, her shrine was a loved place of pilgrimage right through mediaeval times. Feast day: February 3rd.

PART IV

The Church Landscape in Later & Modern Times

Love divine, all loves excelling
   Joy of Heaven, to earth come down,
Fix in us thy humble dwelling,
   All thy faithful mercies crown;
Jesu, thou art all compassion,
   Pure unbounded love thou art:
Visit us with thy salvation,
   Enter every trembling heart.

Come, almighty to deliver,
   Let us all thy grace receive;
Suddenly return, and never,
   Never more thy temples leave.
Thee we would be always blessing,
   Serve thee as thy hosts above,
Pray and praise thee without ceasing,
   Glory in thy perfect love.

Finish then thy new creation,
   Pure and spotless let us be;
Let us see thy great salvation
   Perfectly restored in thee:
Changed from glory into glory,
   Till in Heaven we take our place,
Till we cast our crowns before thee –
   Lost in wonder, love and praise.

                     Charles Wesley

THE CHURCH LANDSCAPE
IN LATER
& MODERN TIMES

THE GENERAL PATTERN: PENZANCE AND DISTRICT

An outline of changes and developments, from the religious and social revolutions of the sixteenth century to the present day, can usefully be gained from a look at the Penzance neighbourhood.

We need to go back to the settlement at Madron chapel with its well (see Madron in Part II). In due course this gave rise to a new, mediaeval church in what is now Madron village or churchtown. We can actually see the progression here, just because of the slight change of location. Usually the new church building directly replaced the old, with no change of position, therefore, for the community either. We are right to assume continuity; but it is not so evident to the eyes.

The old oratory at Madron still remained a revered shrine. But also there was the building of the chapels in a Penzance which had as yet no parish of its own. In the extended concept of the family in mediaeval life, each group – association, guild, hospice, and so on, would seek to centre its life on its own oratory. Indeed, it has been said, though this is an over-simplification, that Penzance itself originally arose from a few fishermen settling near the present pier, and building themselves a chapel dedicated to Saint Anthony. On the little rise of ground just above was the chapel of Saint Mary. The whole is on a small headland between two small bays, and the name *Pen Sans* – Holy Headland – may derive directly from this. However, remembering the Celtic love of headlands, hills and islands, there may well have been an earlier centre of prayer here. In an almost inevitable course of events, the town acquired a seal and arms of the highly popular Saint John the Baptist – the 'holy head' becoming that of the decapitated martyr. Such, sometimes playful, elaborations were popular in mediaeval times. There was also a chapel of Saint Clare (of Assisi or the St Cleer of East Cornwall?) on the way out from Penzance to Madron.

From the mid-sixteenth century we have to distinguish a number of religious denominations, mainly: The Church of England fully established by law early in the reign of Queen Elizabeth I, and Congregationalists, Baptists and English Presbyterians at once claiming independence of the state and the right to follow different forms of worship; later independent bodies – the seventeenth century Society of Friends or Quakers, eighteenth century Wesleyan Methodism, nineteenth century Plymouth Brethren and the Salvation Army, twentieth

40. The original chapel and baptistery at Madron.

century Protestant Pentecostal groups; the bare survival, and then the growth, of Catholicism.

In or near Penzance we can see, or have seen, the following.

Church of England. The chapel of St Mary survived what was otherwise a sweeping away of religious institutions, and continued to serve the community as a subsidiary chapel to Madron parish church. The growth of the town led to the building of the present St Mary's in the first part of the nineteenth century, a period of great importance for Penzance, and it became a parish church in 1871. St Paul's church was built in 1843 through the enthusiasm of a curate of St Mary's; it attained independent parish status, but with recent shrinking in resources of various sorts it now forms one parish with St Mary's. Anglican zeal for church building in Victorian times is further seen in the creation of St John's parish, in a growing area of the town, in 1882. St Mary's parish is responsible for a primary school; there is also a Woodard Trust school for girls.

Free Churches. The first church building actually to be erected after the sixteenth century was the Congregational chapel in Market Jew Street. Built in 1707, it was rebuilt a hundred years later, and maintained its life until after the Second World War, even sending a temporary off-shoot into a new housing estate. However, lack of numbers eventually closed it, and the building has now been incorporated into a large shop of modern design. Perhaps even more significant for those who read signs in the times has been the history of the octagon-shaped chapel built by a break-away Congregational group. After further troubles, it was used by the Baptists, who then themselves removed to their still surviving chapel in Clarence Street, which was built in 1836. At first the Jordan Chapel, as the original had been named, stayed in Baptist hands with a minority congregation. Then it was sold for use as a public hall, which in due course became a cinema. The site is now swallowed up in the Government building which does its best gracelessly to dominate the physical and spiritual skyline.

Various Independent Groups. From 1803 the Society of Friends had a meeting-house in Causewayhead, on the site of what later became St George's Hall, a kind of pleasant local music hall; today, here again the shops have taken over. However, there is a charming Quaker meeting-house at nearby Marazion, the first to be built in Cornwall, in 1688. Elim Pentecostal Hall at the top of Taroveor Road was the most notable building associated with the Pentecostal groups. The Gospel Hall just off New Street opens up a new horizon in that until it was sold to the Plymouth Brethren in 1913 it was the Jewish Synagogue; there is still a small Jewish burial ground in Penzance. The Salvation Army Citadel at the top of Queen Street has also an enriched history; what is now the main part of the building was the first Methodist church to be built in Penzance. Here John Wesley preached in 1789, shortly before he died.

Methodism. John and Charles Wesley both visited Penzance a number of times, and their work in Cornwall had an almost unlimited influence, more than once evoking the comment that, whatever the law might say, Methodism was Cornwall's established church. As the Methodist movement came to be entirely independent, it was necessary to provide permanent places of meeting and worship. These increased in number, not only to house increasing numbers of worshippers, but as new 'connexions' were formed with congregations seeking their own variations in life and worship. Movements towards re-unification followed later, however, culminating in the Reunion in 1932.

The clearest example is perhaps seen in the Bible Christians, also known as Bryanites from their founder William O'Bryan (originally Bryant) of Luxulyan, a devoted local preacher of the Wesleyan Methodist Church. He felt impelled to form an independent body in 1815; but after evangelization in many parts of the world as well as Devon and Cornwall, Bible Christians eventually became part of the United Methodist Church in 1907. The place of worship they built in Penzance is now usually referred to simply as High Street Methodist. Another distinguished Methodist church still in use is in Chapel Street (the street is named after the old St Mary's Chapel, see above) and towards the back of the town is Richmond Methodist Church. Others, however, at Mount Street, Parade Street, Alexandra Road, have fallen victim to a drying up of enthusiasm. The much valued West Cornwall School for Girls also no longer exists; its buildings are now used by Penwith District Council.

The Catholic Church. The Emancipation Act of 1829 lifted all but a very few of the restrictions on the rights of Catholics as British citizens. The first visible sign of this in Cornwall was the completion of the church of the Immaculate Conception of the Blessed Virgin Mary in 1843. This considerable enterprise, supported by all who had a penny to give, was led by the indefatigable Father William Young, who then promptly went on to start work all over again in Bodmin. The Penzance church has responsibility for outlying Mass centres, at St Just in Penwith and the Marazion Cheshire Home, though it has recently withdrawn one from nearby Newlyn. It also serves the charming chapel and priest's dwelling on St Mary's, Isles of Scilly, where visiting or semi-retired clergy often help out. Religious Sisters have made their contributions to the parish and local community, at various times in charge of an orphanage and two schools. Presentation Sisters now care for St Mary's haven for the elderly.

A distinctive mark has been made in the streets of the area lying east of the Catholic church. Towards the end of the nineteenth century, a Mr James Reynolds, having made money out of the Penlee Quarry, invested it in a house-building project. He appointed two trustees: Father Warren Middleton and Mr Francis Harvey of the well known Penzance firm of solicitors. The streets were named by Mr Reynolds after those saints whose names were borne by members of his family: St Catherine (his wife) and the children, St Mary Street, St Dominic Street, St Philip Street, and so on. Mr Harvey was presumably included with a son, and a great saint, in St Francis Street. But there was also a Warren Street to express a particular regard for Father Middleton. This has now acquired the title of St Warren Street. Thus – sometimes – are saints born! It is not for us to doubt that the good father is in Heaven, participating in the prayers of all the saints for church and people on earth. But the first step towards an official recognition would be a spontaneous local devotion to Warren Middleton, of which, so far at least, no signs have been apparent.

CHURCH DEDICATIONS AND DISTINGUISHED PEOPLE

After the sixteenth century there was a great change concerning the public, and indeed private, devotion to the saints. Anglican caution over honouring saints, and still more asking their intercession for us in Heaven, was reflected in the careful selection in the Book of Common Prayer and in the dedications of new Anglican churches. The various independent Churches almost wholly rejected this form of venerating saints. The Catholic sense of the sacramental presence of the holy patron, and the popular devotion it entails, shared with the Orthodox and other Churches of eastern Christendom, do, however, give greater interest and variety to church life. In any case, we need not confine our attention to those entitled 'saint'.

THE CHURCH OF ENGLAND

Dedications of churches built for Anglican worship include, for instance, Holy Trinity at Penponds, Christ Church at Lannarth near Gwennap, and All Saints at Millbrook, and among others: Saint Andrew at Pencoys, Saint Anne at Hessenford, Saint Bartholomew at Porthleven, Saint George at Truro, Saint James at Torpoint, Saint John the Evangelist at Halsetown near St Ives, Saint John the Baptist at Pendeen, Saint Luke at Tideford, the Cathedral Church of

Saint Mary at Truro (taking its name from the mediaeval church on the same site), Saint Michael at Newquay, Saint Peter at Treverbyn and Saint Paul at Charlestown both near St Austell, Saint Stephen at Treleigh by Redruth. At Carbis Bay, the dedication is to Saint Anta and All Saints; at Devoran, Saint Petroc has joined Saint Peter in the traditional manner, while Saint Piran is patron of Carharrack. There are others which repeat some of these dedications; mainly, the churches were erected in growing areas of population affected by nineteenth century industrialisation. These saints are to be found in Part III, except for Anta, Petroc and Piran, who are in Part II.

King Charles the Martyr. This dedication is an original Anglican contribution. The parish church at Falmouth was built in 1662, just after the town of Falmouth itself received its first charter, and also just after the Restoration of the monarchy with King Charles II, and of the Church of England banned under the Commonwealth. During the problems of his reign, by no means all caused by himself, King Charles I had stood, constitutionally and in popular feeling, for the Church of England, and the Church was disestablished with his defeat in the Civil War. His illegal execution in 1649 was as much the result of religious as political factors: he refused to give his seal to the imposition of Presbyterianism. This, with the uprightness of his personal life (his court was both one of the most cultured and most decent in all English history) together with writings in praise of his life and death, evoked his widespread acclaim as a martyr. In 1662, a service for the day of his death, January 30th, was added to the Book of Common Prayer.

41. Interior of the seventeenth century church of King Charles the Martyr at Falmouth.

42. Parson Hawker of Morwenstow in his sea boots.

This particular order of service is no longer in use, but Charles I, King and Martyr, has a place in the Church of England Common Worship Calendar.

Robert Stephen Hawker. The most charismatic figure – using the term in its proper sense – to come out of Anglicanism in Cornwall is the famous Parson Hawker of Morwenstow. Born in Plymouth in 1803, he was educated at Oxford. and married a lady from near Bude. He became vicar of Morwenstow in 1843, and remained there all his life, though finally going to Plymouth as a sick man and dying there in 1875. He is buried in Plymouth cemetery. As with so many of the people whose lives are given in brief in this book, it is hard to do justice to him in a small space. Perhaps it may best be done by indicating his 'completeness'. A man of very marked character, showing itself not least in his dress which combined the parson with the seaman, he was far too constructive in his life and work simply to be described as an eccentric. He devoted himself to his parishioners, helping them in their poverty in very difficult circumstances. In winter, on a perilous coast, the vicar was fully involved in helping the living and burying the dead from shipwreck. He was an encourager of local schooling and farming, a lover of animals and birds, and of course a well known poet. His work was supported by his reverence for Morwenstow, its history and traditions, and the saint whose patronage he claimed. Well might he write of Morwenstow:

> Firm was their faith, the ancient bands,
>   The wise of heart in wood and stone;
> Who reared, with stern and trusting hands,
>   These dark grey towers of days unknown:
> They filled these aisles with many a thought,
>   They bade each nook some truth reveal:
> The pillared arch its legends brought,
>   A doctrine came with roof and wall . . .
>
> Still points the tower, and pleads the bell;
>   The solemn arches breathe in stone;
> Window and wall have lips to tell
>   The mighty faith of days unknown.
> Yea flood, and breeze, and battle-shock
>   Shall beat upon this church in vain:
> She stands, a daughter of the rock,
>   The changeless God's eternal fane.

METHODISM AND BIBLE CHRISTIANS IN CORNWALL

Methodist churches have been largely known by their location, the village itself or the street of a larger town. But the human instinct to give significant titles to important buildings has not been lacking. Centenary, as at Camborne, commemorates the hundred years from 1739 when John Wesley began his 'field preaching'. The use of Biblical place-names was especially popular among Bible Christians; Billy Bray's chapel at Baldhu was Bethel – the House of God, the site of Jacob's Heavenly Ladder. Usually these are Old Testament; but there is the touching Bethany, the home of Mary, Martha and Lazarus, at Doddycross in the country not far from Liskeard. Trinity is occasionally found, as at Wadebridge. There has been an increasing tendency to use the commemoration of Wesley himself; the name, for instance, was always employed at Redruth church, while St Columb Wesleyan church has become St Columb Wesley church. (There was a Billy Bray memorial chapel at Carharrack, now closed.) A certain number of saints' names have also come into use. St Clement's at Mousehole reflects St Clement's Isle just off the little porth; St Luke's at Bolventor reminds us that there was once a mediaeval chapel of that dedication there. St Mary's at Par is in the Anglican parish under the Blessed Virgin's patronage. In Truro, also, is St Mary Clement, next door to the cathedral and the home also of the one-time congregation of a chapel in St Clement Street. (St George's is now kindly leased to St Michael's Catholic Small School.) Reorganization after the Methodist Union in 1932 brought combinations, and the need to think about church names; and it appears to be then that Troon, St Austell and Padstow chose Saint John the Evangelist. These are to be found in Part III.

43. Portrait bust of John Wesley at Altarnun.

John and Charles Wesley. John Wesley was born in 1703, and after a long apprenticeship in the religious life, he began his field-preaching in 1739. He had found that it was not possible in the structure of the Established Church fully to pursue his vocation: 'To promote as far as I am able vital practical religion and by the grace of God to beget, preserve, and increase the life of God in the souls of men'. In 1743 he first came to Cornwall, and not far over the border he was given hospitality at the cottage of Digory and Elizabeth Isbell at Trewint. The cottage itself is just off the main road (A30) and can be visited as a Methodist shrine where we can see The Prophet's Chamber, the simple two-room addition built on by the devoted couple for use by John Wesley and other Methodists. The old Methodist church of nearby Altarnun bears over the doorway a carving of the head of Wesley made in 1836 by the distinguished Cornish sculptor N.N. Burnard.

Places where John Wesley preached during his repeated visits are sometimes marked by name, most notably perhaps the Wesley Rock which gave its name to part of what is now more usually referred to as Heamoor, between Penzance and Madron. Here, the rock on which he stood in the open air was preserved inside the chapel when it was built, and later moved the few yards so that, with its inscription, it forms the focus of preaching for the newer and larger chapel next door. Most famous of all is Gwennap Pit, the circular 'saucer' in the ground near Redruth, which in 1806 was enlarged as a memorial of John Wesley to hold a congregation of two thousand people. The great occasion here is the service once held on Whit Monday, though now, due partly to a secularist government, on the Spring Bank Holiday, when the pit is filled with enthusiastic people. The style of worship is different, but perhaps there is a kinship of spirit with those Cornish audiences/congregations who filled the round playing-places for the celebrations of mediaeval times. Portraits of John Wesley were very popular, including busts made of pottery to be found on many a mantelpiece. All these things are witness to John Wesley as a truly charismatic figure, one venerated as a present, living influence in a manner not far from the traditional veneration of the saints. Of recent times there has been from Methodist sources a very sympathetic comparison of John Wesley with Saint Petroc. He died in 1791.

At Gwennap Pit, everywhere in Methodist circles, and of course far beyond, are sung the hymns of Charles Wesley. In the great and ancient tradition of Christian hymnody in being *both* emotional and doctrinal, these hymns established the living religion evoked by his brother in the minds and hearts of his listeners with an effectiveness which can only be achieved by music 'married to immortal verse'. Charles Wesley, who was born in 1707 and died in 1788, actually set foot in Cornwall a few weeks before his brother. (Typically of the spread of a religious movement, they came not as the very first 'apostles' but in response to a spirit already moving among Cornish people.) Methodism was for long acutely suspicious of a seen beauty in religion, in ritual, in colour, in the popularization of 'images', even so simple and basic a form as the cross. It was above all through Charles Wesley that a richness of life came through hymns and therefore music. These played a great role, along with the words of the Bible and the vivid exhortations of the preacher, so that many a man and woman might say of religious music, borrowing the words of Milton, that it did:

> Dissolve me into ecstasies,
> And bring all Heaven before mine eyes.

Billy Bray. Cornish Methodism, encouraged by the system of Local Preachers, produced some remarkable men and women preachers of the Gospel. Among the most vivid personalities were those to be found in the Bible Christian movement, including Catherine and Mary, wife and daughter of William O'Bryan himself.

Best remembered and best loved must be William or Billy Bray, who was born at Twelveheads in the parish of Kea, near Truro, in 1794 and died at the ripe age of seventy-four in 1868 after an amazing lifetime of activity. He is buried in Baldhu churchyard. A certain extra liveliness about the Bible Christian spirit became in Billy Bray an enormous, childlike humour and gaiety. A poor mine worker, he discovered in the process of his conversion that he, like all brethren

44. Portrait of a remarkable
     man, Billy Bray . . .

45. . . . and his memorial in
     Baldhu churchyard.

in Jesus Christ, was the King's Son: indeed – and we may be reminded of the child's way of Saint Thérèse of Lisieux – the King's little boy. Laughing, singing and dancing are normal enough in the religious life of cultures more natural than that of modern industrialism, and are certainly as expressive of the life of the Spirit as a sober cheerfulness. But from the open-hearted gaiety and complete lack of self-consciousness of so many saints we move to the especial, though not unique, characteristics of Billy Bray when we hear of him carrying a clerical gentleman round the dining-room table to a chair, and then he himself rolling on the floor, in joy at the news of the 'conversion' of the household. What is sometimes overlooked in this well known anecdote is the purity of Billy's religion. He may take unexpected physical action: there is none of the aura of self-righteousness, the spiritual impertinence, sometimes associated with those, in a number of Christian bodies, who claim to be moved by the Spirit. Simply: 'Converted, be ye?' – 'Yes, thank God.' – 'Be the missus converted?' – 'Yes.' – 'Thank the dear Lord.' That is all.

Of course the last person to be offended by laughter was Billy himself. He was a living denial of the assumption, which has become only too prevalent, that religion is something grave and apart. (Significant has been the change in the meaning of 'solemn' – correctly speaking, Christmas is a solemn feast, i.e. a great and joyful celebration.) In his preaching tours, Billy Bray would walk as much as twenty miles on a Sunday, and on weekdays he combined periods of preaching with the shifts at the mine: 'I have worked twenty hours in the twenty-four, and had not the Lord helped me I could not have done it'.

With this, he managed to grow vegetables in the cottage garden, for he had a wife and five children to support. His family life had changed so much since the time when he had been a thoughtless drunkard. They became involved in his activities, for it was a very united family, and the children must have found it a good deal more fun than going to school. As Billy said of the first three chapels which he – literally – built: 'The Lord put it into my head to build a chapel . . . so my little son and me went to work and got some stone . . .'

INDEPENDENTS AND THE RELIGIOUS SOCIETY OF FRIENDS

Hugh Peters. The religious powers of the Commonwealth – Congregationalist, Baptist and Presbyterian, were no more tolerant of unauthorized preachers and teachers than any other government. However when, in 1655, George Fox was imprisoned for eight months in the gaol of Launceston Castle, Oliver Cromwell did send a representative to enquire into reports of the bad conditions in which the prisoner was being held.

Not much came of it, but this man was the Reverend Hugh Peters or Peter (1598-1660) whose father (originally Thomas Dykewood) came from near Fowey and whose mother was Martha Treffry of Place. Early a supporter of the Congregationalists and Independents, Hugh Peters had a notable career in the Netherlands and New England (he was a trustee in the foundation of Harvard

University). Returning to England, he played a leading role during the Commonwealth, and at the restoration of the Monarchy he was one of those whom King Charles II's distaste for vengeance could not save from swift execution. His striking variety of interests and aptitudes included those in war, commerce, politics, scholarship, religious controversy, and a broader religious devotion – notably sharing in the Catholic love and veneration of the Sacred Heart of Jesus. Nor did he ignore the concerns of his home and his Cornish relatives; and when we read of 'Hugh Peters, fervidest of Puritans, staunchest and jolliest of army chaplains', perhaps we may remember a later remark: 'praising the Lord in the Cornish style with a loud voice'.

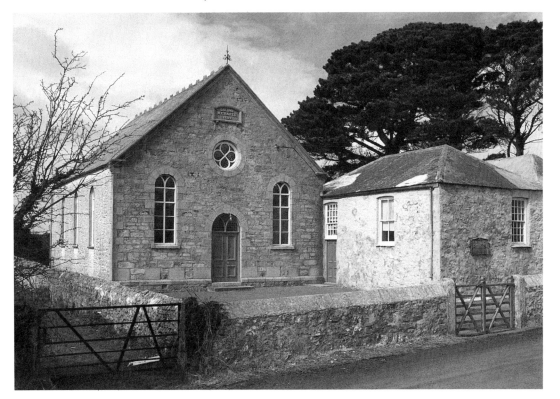

46. Billy Bray's chapel at Baldhu.

Loveday Hambly. Seventeenth century prisons may have been less hygienic than contemporary ones, but they were more open. In Launceston gaol in 1655, George Fox was able to lead a number of his visitors into becoming members of the Friends of the Truth, as they called themselves in the early days. Outstanding was Loveday Hambly, widow of a gentleman farmer of Tregangeeves, in the St Austell parish but opposite St Mewan across what is now the A390 road. (A widening of this road was recently permitted to destroy the Quaker burial ground there.)

This 'saint – a Quaker saint', as she has been described, was already a devout woman of about fifty when she met George Fox. She became the central figure in the Quaker life in Cornwall. Tregangeeves was a place of hearty welcome, friendship and inspiration, where important decisions were taken over the life and organization of the Friends, and to which guests journeyed from up the country. 'We came to Loveday Hambly's . . .' is the repeated phrase in reports and accounts. George Fox himself went there more than once, and links were drawn still closer when his stepdaughter, Mary Fell, became the second wife of Mistress Hambly's beloved nephew and adopted son, Thomas Lower.

Like many gentlewomen of her time, she ran a large and complex household with expertise and humanity: 'More a mother to me than a mistress' is the witness of one of her servants. The real strength which lay in her dominant personality (they do not always go together) is the cheerful fortitude with which she bore considerable suffering. Quaker defiance of the law over such things as unauthorized preaching in public and refusal to pay church tithes brought her various penalties, from seizure of her best cattle to repeated terms of imprisonment, sometimes for a month at a time. Yet this theoretically ageing gentlewoman maintained her active life for over twenty-five years. When she died in 1682 she had left a permanent mark on the development of the Society of Friends.

47. The Friends' Meeting House at Come-to-Good near Feock, built in 1703, twenty-one years after the death of Loveday Hambly.

CATHOLIC LIFE AND WORSHIP

Namings. A surprising name to be applied to the Cornish landscape in later times on the south-west of Bodmin Moor is **St Bellarmine's Tor**. Presumably the small chapel, of which there are still a few signs on the top of the tor, was originally that of a Celtic saint. But it has been suggested that there was a mediaeval dedication to Saint Bartholomew, which is that at Warleggan not far away, where it is said the common pronunciation of the saint's name somewhat resembles Bellarmine. The latter name became familiar through the fat, stoneware pots, with a distorted human face mocking Cardinal Robert Bellarmine, exported from Flanders in the early seventeenth century. His own methods of controversy were marked by charity and reasonableness, but he was notorious among Protestant communities as the leading Catholic spokesman in the public religious arguments, and a Jesuit at that. Some of Saint Robert Bellarmine's writings on Christian life and doctrine were available (though illegally) in England, and one book was published in Welsh.

Dedications. In 1794 a community of English-speaking Carmelite nuns fled from Antwerp in the face of the French revolutionary armies, and were given his manor house at Lanherne by the Earl of Arundell. The public chapel there was dedicated to Saint Joseph (see below) and Saint Anne (see Part III). An early nineteenth century church building at Falmouth – designed to look like a private house on the outside, and also made acceptable to the authorities through high-placed French interest in the French and Breton fishermen coming to the port – was dedicated to Saint Mary Immaculate ('free of all sin').

The freedom since 1829 has brought many churches, with a wide variety of dedications. Newquay gives us Holy Trinity and Perranporth Christ the King, while at Padstow Our Saviour is joined by Saint Petroc, and at St Ives (under the title of the Sacred Heart, see Hugh Peters) by Saint Ia. The Blessed Virgin Mary is celebrated under a number of titles: for example, Our Lady of Victories at Callington, her Assumption into Heaven at Redruth and, at Saltash, Our Lady of Perpetual Succour, deriving from the world-famed, world-loved and world-copied icon in Rome. She is patron of Helston church where, unfortunately, she is not joined by Saint Michael. However, Saint Petroc joins Our Lady at Bodmin church as does Saint Nectan at Hartland, Saint Piran at Truro, Saint Neot at Liskeard and Saint Nicholas at Looe. Classic dedications are found at St Agnes (the same saint), Bude (Saint Peter), Camborne (Saint John the Baptist), Tintagel (Saint Paul), Mullion, Wadebridge and Hayle Hospital (Saint Michael).

These can be found in Parts II and III. The following are other patrons of local Catholic churches, with a brief study of Saint Cuthbert Mayne, of particular Cornish interest.

Anthony of Padua. The Saint joining Our Lady, Star of the Sea, at St Mawes was intended to be Saint Anthony of Egypt (see Part III) with especial reference to St Anthony Lighthouse on the Point, sending out its beams across troubled waters. However, somewhere in the proceedings he was assumed to be the Franciscan friar of Portugal, who worked among the Muslims of Morocco, in France and in Italy, being buried in Padua, and canonized a mere year later in 1232. The numerous statues of this saint show him carrying a Bible, a lily and the

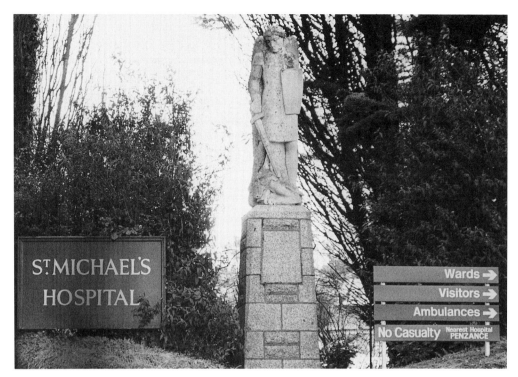

48. Angels and saints of traditional fame are still patrons
of very practical good works (Hayle).

Christ Child, signifying his deep learning, beautiful teaching and tender love. He
is of course famous above all for the aid given to those who have lost things of
any kind; the most remarkable response to 'Saint Anthony find ...' known to
this writer being that of a contact lens knocked into the sands of Gwithian
Towans. Feast day: June 13th.

Augustine and Monica. The Catholic church at St Austell is dedicated to Saint
Augustine of Hippo, with his mother Saint Monica. This was formerly
administered by Canons Regular of the Lateran from Bodmin. Like many other
religious communities of both men and women, their rule of life is based on that
outlined by their patron and 'father', Augustine, a rule which has been hardly less
influential than that of Saint Benedict (see Part III). His writings have been
equally influential, notably his *Confessions* and *The City of God*, which speak
especially to our times, so like his in world disruption and spiritual confusion.
Even as this great bishop lay dying in AD 430, in Hippo the centre of his North
African diocese, the destroying Vandals were at the gates. Feast day: August 28th.

It is her own son who tells us about Saint Monica; and it is he who likens the
role of parents, in their love and self-sacrifice, their authority and wise management,
to that of a bishop and his flock. As so often happened at the time, the family was
a mixture of baptized and unbaptized. Monica's husband eventually became a
Christian, but died when Augustine, the eldest of three children, was eighteen.
She followed Augustine's intellectually proud and somewhat licentious career
with prayers and tears, and did so more literally when she insisted on following

him from Roman North Africa to Italy. Milan's great bishop, Saint Ambrose, befriended both of them, and in due course received Augustine into the Christian Church. Monica, patron of widows and mothers, died soon after, in 837, when she and Augustine were on the journey home. Her feast day is now a day before his: August 27th.

Edward the Confessor. The term Confessor pays tribute to King Edward: a confessor bears witness to Christ in an especial way in his life, as the martyr does in the manner of his death. It is difficult to do justice to this great king, who was patron of England until the adoption of Saint George (see Part III). Coming to the throne in 1042, he dealt with the troubles of his reign with a determined gentleness sometimes misunderstood by later, coarse-grained, historians; and he left a number of legacies to his country. His love of justice was enshrined in an oath, naming him, their royal predecessor, which was taken by succeeding monarchs for many centuries. The miracles of his life-time lingered on in the tradition of 'touching for the King's Evil': the hope that the touch of a king's hand would bring about the curing of scrofula. At the site of the already revered Benedictine monastery at Westminster he built the first great abbey church, and established the centre of government to which the present Houses of Parliament have succeeded, and of law (Westminster Hall). His burial place – uniquely not destroyed by Henry VIII, no doubt chary of encouraging attacks on royalty – is once more a shrine of pilgrimage in the Abbey. It is also happy that a recently built Catholic church in Mawnan Smith, in the countryside of south Cornwall, should remember this Englishman. Feast day: October 13th.

Joan of Arc. With evident suitability, she is patron of the church at Torpoint, a town which has grown in association with the naval and military centre of Plymouth. Her story is famous, but some of the most interesting facts are not always emphasized. This girl of seventeen or eighteen arrived at the royal court, claiming a divine call to lead the armies of France when all was in disarray. Not only the character and inspiration of Joan but something of the times reveal themselves in her success. As Donald Attwater remarked, in the 1940s, 'In our so-called emancipated times, she would have been put in the WRAC and allowed to drive a truck'. The verdict at the trial – ostensibly for heresy and witchcraft, and in itself fairly conducted – was a political one, demanded by the English and their allies. This verdict was quashed by a papal commission of enquiry twenty-five years after her execution by burning in 1431. A girl 'of the people', with typical practical sense and down-to-earth humour, she was a real soldier who really loved 'the enemy', spending the night after a battle caring for all the wounded, bringing God's comfort to all the dying. Jeanne was canonized in 1920. Thus a saint had been raised up for later times, with our nationalistic wars involving masses of 'ordinary' men and women as never before. Feast day: May 30th.

Joseph. The patron saint of the churches at Gunnislake and Hayle can surely be regarded – Our Lady, Saint Mary apart – as the greatest of them all. The Gospels give us vivid perceptions into the man who was called to be father, with every earthly attribute except physical paternity, to God walking this earth, and to be husband, in every way except in the begetting of children, to the young woman who gave bodily existence to Him, truly God becoming also truly Man.

Saint Matthew tells us of the formal betrothal of the 'just man' Joseph and Mary, and, on his realisation that she was already with child, his decision to

49. The shrine of Saint Joan of Arc in the Catholic church at Torpoint.

protect his wife from public shame, let alone the Jewish penalty of stoning to death. Then he has the first of his angelic dreams, when he learns that the child is conceived of the Holy Spirit, and the son is to be Jesus – the Saviour. Saint Luke tells how Joseph, of the House of David, has to go to Bethlehem for the highly organized Roman census, and of the birth of the child, the wondrous worship of the shepherds, the fulfilling of the law in circumcision and the offering of the first-born son in the Temple, where he is hailed by the aged and devout Simeon and Anna. Matthew takes up the account with the worship of the gentile Wise Men, and appearance of an angel to Joseph instructing him to 'take the child and His mother, and flee to Egypt' away from the murderous intent of King Herod. He was inspired in due course to return to the land of Israel, but to go to its northern parts, to settle in Nazareth. We hear again of this guardian of the childhood of Christ on the occasion of the pilgrimage to Jerusalem for the Passover Feast when the boy was twelve, entering the first stage of growing up. Very significant are the words when the missing lad has been discovered among the Jewish teachers in the Temple: 'Your father and I have been anxiously seeking you.' – 'How was this? Didn't you know that I must be in my Father's house?'

Obedient to Mary and Joseph, Jesus grew up to be known as the carpenter's son and, indeed, himself as carpenter. We hear nothing more of Joseph and so it is assumed that he died before Our Lord began his ministry, and certainly before, on the cross, he entrusted his Mother and his friend John to each other's care. Dying in that home in Nazareth, Joseph is named patron of a happy death, and he is world-wide guardian of families of all kinds, including religious houses, educational institutions, and other enterprises.

The older Feast day is March 19th, which always falls in Lent. There is now also a feast of Saint Joseph the Workman (rather than Worker) on May 1st. This links with the natural festivities of May Day, while at the same time blessing all human labour and artistry, in contrast with the political and class hostility too often disfiguring that day.

SAINT CUTHBERT MAYNE AND
HIS CIRCLE

Launceston gaol has held other prisoners of conscience as well as George Fox. Most pathetic, perhaps, was Agnes Prest from the parish of Boyton in north Cornwall. Regarding her as a 'mazed creature', the authorities under Queen Mary Tudor were unwilling to punish her further for her hysterical attacks on certain Catholic beliefs. But after her release from Launceston, she made her way to Exeter where her public outcries caused her to be arrested again, and after trial, she suffered the penalty of burning to death in that city. She was the only Cornish victim of the measures initiated by Queen Mary, in a period when what had been occasional practices of the Middle Ages were being turned into common tools of government.

In the following reign of Elizabeth I, Cuthbert Mayne found himself in

51. Saint Cuthbert Mayne,
by Father Michael Reid.

Launceston gaol. Of a yeoman's family near Barnstaple, he was sent to Oxford university, became chaplain to St John's College, and came into contact with other distinguished members of that college, notably Edmund Campion, eventually executed at Tyburn in 1581, and Gregory Martin, a major translator of the Catholic English Bible known as the Douay version. At home in the west country, and hearing of a warrant out for his arrest at Oxford, he took ship from a Cornish port for the continent. Trained as a Catholic priest ('secular' priest, not a Jesuit) he returned to minister in Cornwall, where he lived under the guise of the steward in the handsome Golden Manor near Probus. This was in 1576. In 1570 Pope Saint Pius V had issued his Bull, or official letter, of a type which could have been more relevant in the conditions of earlier centuries, excommunicating Queen Elizabeth and releasing Catholics from their duty of loyalty to the present monarch. The latter was only by way of a recommendation, but it served to concentrate attacks on the Catholic community by those whose inflamed sense of patriotism was added to religious hostility and the attraction of gaining the

50. The relic – part of the skull – of Cuthbert Mayne is carried in procession at a Saint Cuthbert Mayne pilgrimage at Launceston.

wealth and property forfeited by the condemned.

Thus, on his arrest by Richard Grenville, the new sheriff of Cornwall, after some months in gaol Saint Cuthbert was brought to trial on charges which included that of high treason. Even within the Elizabethan statute his legal defence was sound enough for the court, judges and jurymen, to be uncertain of their verdict. However, the man who was knighted for this work, Sir Richard Grenville, obtained confirmation of the guilty verdict from London. Cuthbert Mayne was hung, drawn and quartered in Launceston market place on November 30th, 1577. This is of course Saint Andrew's Day, and Saint Cuthbert's feast is on November 29th. Such missionary priests were forbidden, and had no wish, to take part in politics; the martyr is commemorated by the dedication of the Catholic church, with its shrine, and a plaque in Launceston castle.

Francis Tregian, the father. The owner of Golden Manor lost his extensive Cornish lands to Sir George Carey, later to become Lord Chamberlain of the Royal Household and patron of the group of players which included William Shakespeare. Tregian, too, was imprisoned for a time in Launceston, but was taken to London where he spent twenty-one years in the Fleet Prison. After a while his wife, Mary, was allowed to live with him there. This indefatigable lady had been turned out of Golden one night and, taking the young children in panniers on her horse, and giving birth to another on the way, had made her way to London. Eventually Francis Tregian was permitted to retire abroad, and he went to live in a house of the Jesuits, San Roque (or St Rock – see also under Gonand in Part II) at Lisbon. He came to be regarded as a man of unusual holiness, and to this day local people bring candles and flowers to his burial-place in the church there.

The evidence of his sanctity is now being closely examined: he is noted for the whole-hearted forgiveness of the enemies who laid waste the life of himself and his family. The cause for his beatification (first step to canonization) has been opened.

Francis Tregian, the son. The most distinguished of many children, Francis the younger, whose parents had sent him abroad, returned to England as head of the family on his father's death in 1608. He made some headway in recovering the Cornish estates, but the crippling fines on those refusing to make the public gesture of submission to the Church of England brought him to the Fleet Prison. There, until his death in 1619, he was able to maintain some of the cultural interests of his family. He himself copied out a great collection of contemporary music by such composers as William Byrd, John Dowland and Peter Philips (compatriots in religion), Giles and Richard Farnaby (of a Truro family) and Thomas Tomkins (of a Lostwithiel family). Part of this manuscript is known as the Fitzwilliam Virginal Book from its lodging in the Fitzwilliam Museum in Cambridge; two other sections, in the British Library and the New York Public Library, include many motets and madrigals.

Nicholas Roscarrock. Another manuscript – of particular interest to a study of the Saints of Cornwall – at present at Cambridge (in the University Library) is Nicholas Roscarrock's 'Catalogue of the Saints of Great Britain'. (See under Endelienta in Part II.) Roscarrock had known Cuthbert Mayne at Oxford and was one of the group of masters and servingmen arrested with him at Golden, where they had gathered to celebrate the feast of Corpus Christi. He, too, was imprisoned for a time in Launceston gaol. Re-arrested in London in the company of another martyr priest, Saint Ralph Sherwin, he was at one time in the Fleet Prison with Francis Tregian the elder, and at another in the Tower with Sir John Arundell. A man of great inner dedication and fortitude, he survived the racking to which he was subjected in a vain attempt to elicit information about Catholic activities. Being finally released after some years, he spent the rest of his long life with congenial friends at Naworth castle near Carlisle, working on his lives of the saints and in contact with such scholars as Camden and Richard Carew.

PART V

Notes on the Isles of Scilly

The Chi/Rho and Celtic Crosses in Cornwall

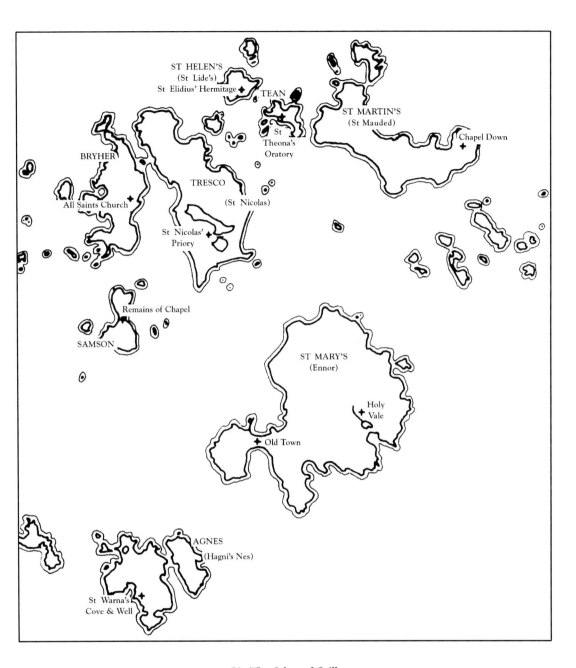

52. The Isles of Scilly

135

NOTES ON THE ISLES OF SCILLY

St Mary's. Previously Ennor (meaning uncertain), the later mediaeval name is derived from the dedication of the church in the Old Town to Our Lady. She is patron, too, of the later Anglican church and – as *Steren an Mor*, Star of the Sea – of the present Catholic chapel. (See Part III.) The source of the name of the serene valley Holy Vale is not known.

Agnes. Various suggestions are made for the original of this name, deriving probably from the Norse of the Vikings who infested the Islands. However, the beautiful and popular Roman Saint Agnes has become patron. (See Part III.) St Warna's Cove marks the landing-place of an Irish maiden who, typically of Celtic saints, sailed herself across the sea in a little boat. The nearby well of the Saint, close to which she presumably lived and prayed, is the only holy well now known on the Islands.

St Martin's. Originally Mauded, the name is very like the old Breton Mawded who is the Cornish Saint Mawes. There is a tradition that Saint Mawgan was once Bishop of the Isles of Scilly, but this can hardly be a trace of his name. (See Part II.) The transition to Saint Martin, a great saint of early times, and extremely popular, is natural enough. (See Part III.)

Tresco. An earlier, though hardly the oldest, name for this Island was St Nicholas – patron of seagoers. The Benedictine Priory established there from the great Abbey of Tavistock in 1114 was also placed under his patronage. (See Part III.) There is no direct connection with the title of abbey given to the nineteenth century mansion of the Dorrien Smith family.

Bryher. No earlier Christian history has survived in names or buildings on this island. However, the Anglican church does much to make up for this in its dedication, not to this or that one, but to All Saints.

Samson. Some have connected this name with the Norse of the Vikings. But the island was certainly known as St Samson, whether the connection with this celebrated Welsh saint, who went to Cornwall, Brittany and the Channel Isles, was by personal visit or holy fame. (See Part II.) The island was of course inhabited until recently.

Tean. Not so long uninhabited, with reminders of life in much earlier times. The name is that of – in Latin form – Sancta Theona. There are remains of the buildings where she lived and worshipped, and of a graveyard dating from this same sixth century period of the Celtic saints.

St Helen's. This name came into use *via* sixteenth century map making. But the saintly mother of Emperor Constantine the Great, pilgrim to Jerusalem and finder of the True Cross, who died about AD 330, has not obscured Saint Elidius. On St Lide's, as the island has been called, the remains still tell us of early monastic life and the honouring of his burial-place. Celtic religious life did not dry up after the great age of the saints, and such men and women may have a very direct effect on history. It was in about 980 that Olaf Tryggvason came to Scilly. As Snorri Sturluson recounts in his Saga, this marauding Viking met Saint Elidius and heard of 'the God of the Christians' and 'agreed to be baptized . . . with all his following'. When he returned to Norway, he 'took with him three priests and other learned men'. As King of Norway he began work there which was taken up by his successor, Saint Olaf. (See Part III.)

THE CHI/RHO AND CELTIC CROSSES IN CORNWALL

1. & 2. The Chi/Rho cross, or monogram on the first two letters of the Greek Christos, Christ – XP, speedily became a Christian sign and emblem throughout the Roman Empire. Here are two common forms.

3. & 4. They are often on a circular plaque, or within the Classical wreath of victory, signifying divine triumph, eternal life.

5. With time, the Rho often became almost assimilated into the cross, as at St Just in Penwith.

6. This form within a circle is notable at St Ninian's Christian centre at Whithorn (Scotland).

7. A round-headed stone may also contain a simple cross, as at St Breward.

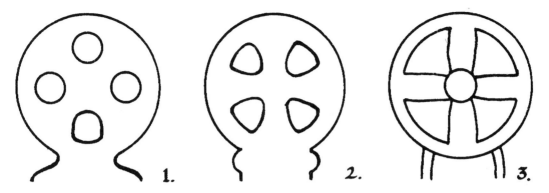

1. Basic round-headed cross forms can be made by cutting through the stone, as in St Piran's cross

2. or in unpierced form, as at St Cleer.

3. A rather more developed common incised type can be seen at Gwithian.

4. A very well-known Celtic style, resembling a Maltese cross, is found at Lanivet.

5. There is an example of skilled Celtic knot-work at Cardinham.

6. The body, or corpus, is sometimes portrayed, both on a simple design or, as at Phillack, set within a pattern.

SOME SOURCES OF INFORMATION

INDEX

SOME SOURCES OF INFORMATION

It is impossible to detail the multitude of ways in which historical information comes to us. The following outline gives basic sources especially, though not only, for the Celtic Saints of Cornwall.

Various Sources

Place Names
1. Use of the name and title, often in partially anglicized form; for example, St Erth.
2. Occasionally the use of the name alone; for example, Mullion.
3. The use of the name with *lan*. This word refers to a place of permanent religious settlement, sometimes a monastery, but essentially a place set apart (cf. Latin sanctuary and Greek *temenos*). The saint is not invariably Celtic: Launceston is derived from *Lan-Stefan* or Stephen. Lanteglos employs *eglos*, church; it has been suggested that the original here is *nans*, valley, though we cannot make a rule that *lan* must be attached to a personal name.
4. The early English *stow*, for example in Davidstow in north-east Cornwall, has much the same connotation as *lan*.
5. *Lok*, more precisely than *lan* the dwelling-place of a particular holy person; as in Luxulyan, Sulian's home and place of prayer.
6. *Merther*, martyr, may well indicate the place of martyrdom as well as the nature of the saint (see under Coan in Part II).
7. Church dedications that are not the same as the name of the civil community; for example, Saint Uny at Redruth.

British, Celtic and Early English Writings
De Excidio Britonum: The History of Britain, from the coming of the Romans to his own time by Saint Gildas (who died about 570).
The Life of Saint Samson (see Part II).
The Life of Saint Paul Aurelian (see Part II).
More generally: the writings of Saint Patrick, Constantius' *Life of Saint Germanus*, Nennius' *History of the Britons*, Saint Bede's *Ecclesiastical History of the English People*.

141

Mediaeval Lives of the Saints and Liturgies

Lives were composed at very varying times, and are valuable in many ways, as including historical facts, witnesses to traditions and to the riches of popular veneration.

Calendars, lives and prayers for saints' feast days are found in surviving church service books or remnants thereof; for example from Bodmin, Launceston priory, Hartland abbey and Exeter cathedral.

A Note on 'Tradition' and 'Legends'

Tradition is:
(a) What is embodied in the life of the Church as it develops down the centuries; complementary to, not opposed to, Holy Scripture.
(b) As tradition or traditions: beliefs and customs well-founded and long-held, but usually by local communities, and not taught authoritatively by the universal Church.
(c) Similar to the above, but closer to what is popularly meant by 'legends'.

Legends, strictly speaking, are written accounts. But the term is more commonly used to signify popular tales, often passed on by word of mouth, in songs and poems, also plays and pictures. As a natural expression of human enjoyment of religion, they have a real value, though their extreme proliferation has to be controlled from time to time. In Cornwall some of these lingered on for a long time after the sixteenth century.

Other Records and Witnesses

Plays and Poems. *Bewnans Meryasek* has survived in Cornwall (see Meryadoc in Part II), as has the cycle of Biblical plays known as the **Ordinalia**, which of course includes some Biblical saints. Similarly, they appear in the poem on the Passion and Resurrection of Christ, **Passyon agan Arluth**.

Hymns and Songs. The sixteenth century break seems to have been decisive in the loss of such compositions celebrating the Cornish saints. There has been a recent revival in formal hymns, but we are still awaiting new folk songs.

Popular Celebrations. A very few have survived, or been revived; see under Petroc in Part II and Michael in Part III.

Church Buildings, their Treasures and Adornment. See for example under Clether, Madron, Piran, as well of course as mediaeval parish churches, and comments on Holy Wells in Part I. For adornment, for example under Ludgvan, Morwenna, Neot and Piala in Part II. For shrines, see Part I and under Endelienta in Part II; for saint's Bells, Part I again.

Travellers and Observers

William of Worcester (1415-1482?) chronicler and traveller. In 1478 he journeyed from Norwich to St Michael's Mount; he gives valuable accounts of what he saw in various Cornish parishes, such as tombs of local saints, and pictured glass in the churches.

John Leland or Leyland (1506?-1552) an official historian to King Henry VIII; his 'Itinerary' through the counties, reaching to Cornwall, had the aim of gathering historical material at a time when much, both manuscripts and buildings, was being lost.

Richard Carew of Antony (1555-1620); his *Survey of Cornwall*, 1602, includes references to surviving folk customs concerning a few saints.

Scholars and Researchers

The Bollandists. A permanently established group of Jesuit scholars, working on the vast field of lives of the saints, founded about 1630 by John Bolland, with their house of studies now in Brussels. The late Paul Grosjean SJ, himself a Breton, was a recent specialist in Celtic studies.

William Borlase (1695-1772). Rector of Ludgvan, student of local history and antiquities, publishing for example his *Cornish Antiquities* in 1754.

Alban Butler (1710-1773). One time chaplain to the Duke of Norfolk and later President of the English College for Catholic boys at St Omer in France; his *Lives of the Fathers, Martyrs and Other Principal Saints*, the product of thirty years' work, is the most complete presentation of lives of the saints in English. See 'Other Valuable Books' below.

Davies Gilbert (1767-1839). President of the Royal Society and

High Sheriff of Cornwall; published his Parochial History of Cornwall in 1838, and worked on Cornish mediaeval texts.

Sabine Baring-Gould (1834-1924). Rector of Lewtrenchard in Devon; among his voluminous writings is his *Lives of the British Saints* (with John Fisher), a rich collection of traditions with some historical analysis.

Henry Jenner (1848-1934) of St Columb Major and Hayle, and assistant keeper of manuscripts at the British Museum; the greatest among the many distinguished figures in the revival of the Cornish language, which is a study of basic historical value in investigating earlier times.

The Work of Canon Doble

Gilbert Hunter Doble (1880-1945), born in Penzance, and Vicar of Wendron, has been the supreme student of the Celtic saints of Cornwall. His studies of some fifty of these holy men and women draw on the evidence of other Celtic countries, Wales and above all Brittany, mediaeval lives, calendars, church service books, festivals, local customs, traditions, places and place-names; he worked in close contact with other scholars in allied fields and of various nationalities. These appeared individually in the 'Cornish Saints' series of booklets. More recently, they have been collected into six volumes edited by Donald Attwater, under the auspices of the Dean and Chapter of Truro Cathedral, and under the title of *The Saints of Cornwall.*

The Roscarrock Manuscript

Nicholas Roscarrock's *Lives of the Saints: Cornwall and Devon,* edited by Nicholas Orme; Devon and Cornwall Record Society, 1992. This prints the text of all the many relevant lives (see Endelienta, p. 42), with a great deal of introductory matter, commentary, full bibliography, and much else including illustrations. Professor Orme provides information on this important manuscript as a whole; for those with eyesight for the handwriting, there is a microfilm in the Courtney Library at the Royal Cornwall Museum, Truro.

Other Valuable Books

The Saints of Cornwall, Nicholas Orme; Oxford University Press, 2000.

Parochial History of Cornwall by the Cornish scholar, Charles Henderson, first appeared in The Cornish Church Guide (Diocese of Truro) in 1925. Published separately under the title of *The Cornish Church Guide* by Barton D. Bradford of Truro, 1964.

The Kingdom of Dumnonia: Studies in History and Tradition in South Western Britain AD 350-1150, Susan Pearce; Lodenek Press, 1978.

In Search of St Piran, E.W.F. Tomlin; Lodenek Press, 1982.

Saint Endellion, Edwin Stark; Dyllansow Truran, 1983.

The History of Glasney College, James Whetter; Tabb House, 1988.

Francis Tregian: Cornish Recusant, P.A. Boyan and G.R. Lamb; Sheed and Ward, 1955.

Francis Tregian 1548-1608: Elizabethan Recusant, Raymond Francis Trudgian; The Alpha Press, 1998.

The Dark Age Saints of Somerset, John Seal; Llanerch (Lampeter), 1995.

The Brendan Voyage, Tim Severin; Arrow Books, 1971.

A Celtic Miscellany: Translations from the Celtic Literatures, Kenneth Hurlstone Jackson; Penguin Books, 1971.

The Penguin Dictionary of Saints, Donald Attwater with Catherine Rachel John; 3rd edition, 1995.

The Oxford Dictionary of Saints, David Hugh Farmer, 4th edition, 1997.

Butler's Lives of the Saints, revised, enlarged and edited by Herbert Thurston S.J. and (primarily) Donald Attwater; Burns & Oates, preferably the 1956 edition.

A SELECT INDEX

General

Saints and Places with a Similar Name

orate · pro · nobis · sancta · gernow ·